Apprenticeship Patterns

Apprenticeship Patterns
Guidance for the Aspiring Software Craftsman

David H. Hoover and Adewale Oshineye

O'REILLY®

Beijing · Cambridge · Farnham · Sebastopol · Tokyo

Apprenticeship Patterns

by David H. Hoover and Adewale Oshineye

Published by O'Reilly Media, Inc., 1005 Gravenstein Highway North, Sebastopol, CA 95472.

O'Reilly books may be purchased for educational, business, or sales promotional use. Online editions are also available for most titles (*oreilly.com*). For more information, contact our corporate/institutional sales department: (800) 998-9938 or *corporate@oreilly.com*.

Editor:	Mary E. Treseler	**Indexer:**	John Bickelhaupt
Production Editor:	Adam Witwer	**Cover Designer:**	Mark Paglietti
Copyeditor:	Emily Quill	**Interior Designer:**	David Futato
Proofreader:	Sada Preisch	**Illustrator:**	Paul Hoover

October 2009:   First Edition.

Revision History for the First Edition:

2009-09-30	First release
2014-03-14	Second release
2023-01-27	Third release

See *http://oreilly.com/catalog/errata.csp?isbn=9780596518387* for release details.

ISBN: 978-0-596-51838-7

[LSI]

1394484405

*For Heather Corallo. She combines truth and love
to inspire everyone around her to be
their best selves.*
—Dave

*This book is dedicated to the clients and students at
all my consultancy gigs for being open-minded; to
the ThoughtWorkers for the good times and the
bad times; to the other TSEs for being Googley; and
to my friends and family for loving me anyway,
even though they didn't always understand.*
—Ade

CONTENTS

FOREWORD

Twenty-five years ago Kent Beck and I sat in Tektronix's Technical Center cafeteria wondering what impact our privileged access to Smalltalk-80 would have on the world.

Never mind reality, I advised Kent. If we could do anything, what would we do with this knowledge?

"I want to change the way people think about programming," Kent said. I agreed. We both wanted to reverse what we thought had been a wrong turn in the progress of our industry. And, amazingly, we did it.

That device I used back in the cafeteria—the "never mind reality" part—was a pattern that I'd first observed used by my college advisor. He tried it on me just like I used it on Kent. The activity, which I now recognize as a pattern, helped Kent and me dare to imagine far-off goals that might otherwise have seemed audacious. And once imagined, our goals looked more achievable.

I call the thought device a pattern because it solves a problem that we often have: we censor our own ambitions. This book is full of similar devices for a wide range of problems. We say that patterns solve problems. "Never mind reality" solved a problem for Kent and me. It got us thinking big thoughts that stuck with us and let us push through our habitual self-censorship.

You've probably tried the "never mind reality" pattern yourself. If you haven't, give it a try. The strongest patterns are the ones that are applied productively over and over again. Patterns don't have to be new to be useful. In fact, it's better if they are not new. Just knowing the names for established patterns is a big help too. Identifying a pattern lets you discuss it without having to retell the whole story every time.

Leaf through this book. You'll see lots of patterns. Many will be familiar. For any one you might say, "I already have that pattern"—and you probably do. But there are two ways that the written patterns here can help you, even when the solution is common knowledge.

First, the written pattern is more complete. It has been studied, characterized, classified, and explained. You'll find unexpected nuggets in each pattern. Savor these nuggets. They make the patterns you already have more powerful.

Second, the patterns are connected. Each one leads to more. When you find one that you already know, you can follow these connections to other patterns you may not know, or never thought of as working together.

Kent and I mined Smalltalk-80 for patterns, and we found plenty. We pitched the pattern concept to our peers, and launched a small revolution. We changed the way people think about programming. Many dozens of books have since been written about patterns and how to use them.

Our revolution is hardly over. The piecemeal growth of pattern terminology became a foundation for Agile software development methods. Many more dozens of books have subsequently appeared.

So, why this book now? Well, we've overloaded our profession with resources. There is more information available about our revolution than any one person can absorb. Still, some people manage to do it. They internalize all the advice available to them and always seem to have it close at hand. How do they do achieve that level of mastery?

This book is full of patterns for mastering our complex field. Mastering is more than just knowing. It is knowing in a way that lightens your load.

Let me give you an example. If you can't remember the order of arguments to the SUBSTR function, you can look that up on the Internet. Thank goodness for the Internet. It has lightened our load a little. But when you use this book's patterns, when you approach your work always open to improvement, you will find yourself writing a different kind of code, code that doesn't depend on knowing the order of SUBSTR's arguments. You will write programs that soar far beyond SUBSTR. This will lighten your load a lot.

All the advice that has come out of our revolution does not help much until it becomes second nature. The craftsmanship movement in software recognizes that making this stuff second nature isn't, well, second nature. These patterns are a welcome contribution to this progression.

—Ward Cunningham

He who knows not and knows not that he knows not, is a fool — shun him!
He who knows not and knows that he knows not, is unlearned — teach him!
He who knows and knows not that he knows, is asleep — awaken him!
He who knows and knows that he knows, is enlightened — follow him!

—Arab proverb quoted by Lady Isabel Burton (1831–1896) in
The Life of Captain Sir Richard F. Burton

Goals

We have written this book in order to share solutions to the dilemmas that are often faced by inexperienced software developers. We're not referring to technical dilemmas; you're not going to find any Java design patterns or Ruby on Rails recipes in this book. Rather, the dilemmas that we focus on are more personal, concerning your motivation and morale. This book should help you through the tough decisions that you face as a newcomer to the field of professional software development.

Audience

This book is written for the person who has had a taste of software development and aspires to become a great software developer. You may be a web developer or a medical device programmer, or you may be building trading applications for a financial institution. Or perhaps you have just graduated from high school or college knowing that software is your future.

Although this book was written for newcomers, more experienced developers will benefit from its content as well. People with several years of experience may find themselves nodding their heads in recognition of dilemmas they've already faced, and may come away with new insights or at least a new vocabulary to describe the solutions they want to apply for themselves or suggest to their colleagues. Even people with a decade or more of experience—particularly those who may be struggling to navigate their careers—will find inspiration and perspective to counter the siren call of promotion to management.

Process

The idea for this book was first hatched when Stickyminds.com asked Dave to write a column about Software Craftsmanship in early 2005. Since Dave considered himself an (experienced) apprentice at the time, the only topic he felt comfortable writing about was apprenticeship. This got him thinking about what he would want to write on the topic. Around that time, Dave read a blog post by software developer Chris Morris* that quoted guitarist Pat Metheny, and the seed for the pattern language was planted with the concept of "being the worst." The seed quickly grew from Dave's blog† to a private wiki that Dave used to organize the initial patterns. The initial patterns were extracted from Dave's career up to that point (2000–2005).

Understanding that these so-called patterns could not really be called patterns unless they were actually common solutions to common problems, Dave began seeking feedback from colleagues in three forms. First, he began publishing the patterns publicly on his website, soliciting feedback with public comment forms. Second, he began interviewing (mostly via email) thought leaders in the field of software development and getting their opinions on the initial patterns. Third, and most important, Dave began interviewing less-experienced practitioners to test the patterns against their recent experiences. The stories told by the less-experienced practitioners also introduced Dave to new patterns that he hadn't yet encountered, or hadn't recognized in his own experiences. It was during these apprenticeship interviews that Dave interviewed Ade, and by mutual agreement, Ade joined the project as a coauthor.

We (Dave and Ade) interviewed people who live and work in places ranging from Australia to India to Sweden. The settings for our discussions were just as diverse, ranging from comments on LiveJournal to an interview in a beautiful bomb-damaged church in the heart of London's financial district.

---

* *http://clabs.org/blogki/index.cgi?page=/TheArts/BeTheWorst*

† Red Squirrel Reflections. Available at: *http://redsquirrel.com/cgi-bin/dave*.

At the same time, people like Laurent Bossavit, Daragh Farrell, and Kraig Parkinson were brave enough to try out the material in a variety of coding dojos, workshops, and boot camps. They then passed on the feedback they received and we (Dave and Ade) tried our best to incorporate it into our notes.

Later in 2005, we ran a focus group on our patterns at the Pattern Languages of Programs workshop.‡ At PLoP, we were able to present our work to seasoned pattern authors (also known as shepherds) who gave us feedback on the format of our patterns and tested their own experiences as programmers against our assertions.

Around the same time, Mary Treseler of O'Reilly Media contacted us about publishing the patterns and encouraged us to keep writing. She helped us out by doing some editing, and two years later we had an agreement to publish the book. During that time we have spoken with countless colleagues via email, in user groups and conference sessions, or just over lunch about the patterns, and we continue to solicit feedback from the community online at *http:// apprenticeship.oreilly.com*.

The end result is in your hands. It is a work grounded in dozens of interviews with practitioners as well as extensive research into the existing literature on learning, the psychology of optimal performance, and anything we could find on the topic of mastery. As you read further, you will see us cite surgeons, choreographers, and philosophers as well as the usual software luminaries. We believe that there is a lot to be learned from studying high performers in all disciplines.

Organization

A pattern is a named description of a recurring solution to a problem in a given context. The description should give readers a deep enough understanding of the problem to either apply the stated solution to their own context or decide that a particular pattern is not appropriate to their situation.

This book is made up of a few large chapters, each filled with a set of related patterns. The names of the patterns are capitalized (e.g., Breakable Toys), and related patterns are frequently referenced. Each chapter weaves its patterns together and provides an introduction to its themes as well as a section wrapping them up. The book's introduction sets the stage for the pattern language, and the conclusion takes a look at "the big picture" regarding skill, apprenticeship, and mastery in our profession.

‡ *http://hillside.net/plop/2005/group1.html*

Pattern Form

Our pattern form is unusual. If you've read other books of patterns, you will see that we're trying something different here. Compared to most pattern languages, we have fewer sections and less discussion of the resolution of abstract forces and constraints. This form was chosen based on extensive feedback from reviewers and from our workshop at PLoP. Based on that feedback, we believe this simpler structure will make our pattern language more accessible for our target audience.

Our patterns all consist of a context, a problem, a solution, and then a set of one or more actions. The context sets the mood, and the problem statement identifies the problem being solved by the entirety of the pattern. The solution usually begins with a one-sentence resolution for the problem, and then dives into greater detail on the issues involved in applying the solution, along with the pattern's relationships to other patterns and supporting stories and literature.

Toward the end of each pattern is an action section, which describes something concrete you can do immediately if you wish to experience the effect of the pattern. These actions serve as example implementations. They supply exercises you can jump into immediately, without having to worry about the applicability of a pattern to your current situation.

It is important to remember that any pattern is meant to contain a family of solutions to a family of problems within a given context. Patterns are meant to be open to modification to fit your circumstances rather than mechanically applied. So if a pattern doesn't precisely fit your circumstances, or none of the items in the action section seem suitable, then try to extrapolate from the raw materials we provide to see if you can build something useful.

Most of our patterns end with a "See Also" section, pointing to the page numbers for related patterns. This should help steer you away from a linear reading of the book in favor of a meandering path that gives you a deeper appreciation of the relationships between the different patterns.

Usage

> A pattern language gives each person who uses it the power to create an infinite variety of new and unique buildings, just as his ordinary language gives him the power to create an infinite variety of sentences.
>
> —*The Timeless Way of Building*, p. 167

Our goal with this project was to create a language of patterns to help you define your own apprenticeship. We cannot possibly know the context of your situation, so be sure to consider the context and problem statements of each pattern to determine whether it applies to you. The patterns are interconnected, and can be used together to create a more powerful experience. For example, while Find Mentors is an excellent and time-tested pattern all by itself, combining it with Rubbing Elbows is far more powerful. On the other hand, Expose Your Ignorance is more dependent on supporting patterns such as Confront Your Ignorance and Retreat Into Competence, and requires a bit more subtlety to use successfully. As with all pattern languages, you should be careful not to overuse these patterns. Don't look for excuses to use every single pattern, but instead pick and choose the most appropriate set for your situation.

You do not necessarily need to read through the patterns in this book from front to back. When Dave read Christopher Alexander's book *A Pattern Language*, he started in the middle and followed the connections between the patterns, which made for a more interesting learning experience. You may want to simply scan the "context" and "problem" statements of each pattern to find the ones that are relevant to your current situation. Scanning all the patterns in this way should help install some triggers in your mind for future situations, when some of the patterns may suddenly become applicable.

This book was initially written in a wiki, and as such it was never really intended to be read in a linear fashion. The early patterns will make reference to the later patterns and vice versa. This will be challenging, and will require you to actively engage with the material. You can browse it like a website, allowing yourself to be distracted by interesting links and never really knowing if you have read everything. There is nothing wrong with this approach.

Of course, we also understand that some people prefer to read from start to finish. Therefore, we've made an effort in the earlier chapters to minimize forward references, where a pattern refers to another pattern that appears later in the book.

Some people might find that they need to go through the book twice: first, a quick skim to get everything into their heads, and then a second time to connect all the links. This approach is also fine. This book is *not* meant to be used as a reference, but is more like an artist's source book—you can dip into it for inspiration from time to time. You might even invent some new approach to using this book that we haven't thought of. Go ahead. This book is like everything else in the real world: the connections aren't always obvious at first, and every time you come back, you find something new.

Using Code Examples

This book is here to help you get your job done. In general, you may use the code in this book in your programs and documentation. You do not need to contact us for permission unless you're reproducing a significant portion of the code. For example, writing a program that uses several chunks of code from this book does not require permission. Selling or distributing a CD-ROM of examples from O'Reilly books does require permission. Answering a question by citing this book and quoting example code does not require permission. Incorporating a significant amount of example code from this book into your product's documentation does require permission.

We appreciate, but do not require, attribution. An attribution usually includes the title, author, publisher, and ISBN. For example: *"Apprenticeship Patterns* by David H. Hoover and Adewale Oshineye. Copyright 2010 David H. Hoover and Adewale Oshineye, 978-0-596-51838-7."

If you feel your use of code examples falls outside fair use or the permission given above, feel free to contact us at *permissions@oreilly.com*.

Safari® Books Online

 Safari Books Online is an on-demand digital library that lets you easily search over 7,500 technology and creative reference books and videos to find the answers you need quickly.

With a subscription, you can read any page and watch any video from our library online. Read books on your cell phone and mobile devices. Access new titles before they are available for print, and get exclusive access to manuscripts in development and post feedback for the authors. Copy and paste code samples, organize your favorites, download chapters, bookmark key sections, create notes, print out pages, and benefit from tons of other time-saving features.

O'Reilly Media has uploaded this book to the Safari Books Online service. To have full digital access to this book and others on similar topics from O'Reilly and other publishers, sign up for free at *http://my.safaribooksonline.com*.

How to Contact Us

You can contact Dave at *dave.hoover@gmail.com* or visit his home page (*http://redsquirrel.com/dave*) to see what he's up to.

You can contact Ade at *ade@oshineye.com*. His website (*http://www.oshineye.com*) points to his photos, writings, and open source code.

Please address comments and questions concerning this book to the publisher:

O'Reilly Media, Inc.
1005 Gravenstein Highway North
Sebastopol, CA 95472
800-998-9938 (in the United States or Canada)
707-829-0515 (international or local)
707 829-0104 (fax)

We have a web page for this book, where we list errata, examples, and any additional information. You can access this page at:

http://oreilly.com/catalog/9780596518387/

To comment or ask technical questions about this book, send email to:

bookquestions@oreilly.com

For more information about our books, conferences, Resource Centers, and the O'Reilly Network, see our website at:

http://www.oreilly.com

Dave's Acknowledgments

I need to start out by thanking the people who gave me my first opportunities to become a software developer. Irv Shapiro, CEO of Edventions, hired me in April of 2000 at the end of my interview with him. Later that year he introduced me to Steve Bunes, CTO of Edventions and CEO of Risetime Technologies, and both of them guided me through my first excited steps into Perl and programming. When Edventions died the death of many other dot-com startups in April 2001, Steve put in a good word for me at the American Medical Association, where I spent the next three years surviving the aftermath of the dot-bomb. I'll repeat my toast to Irv on the night after he hired me: "Thank you, Irv, for taking a chance on a gentile like me."

Two people at the AMA gave me my first opportunity to move beyond my first language. John Dynkowski saw some potential in me, and recruited me to work on some of the AMA's first J2EE projects. He did this at no small political cost to himself, and he was a constant source of encouragement during the 18 months that I worked in his department. Doug Fedorchak, my immediate supervisor, gave me the autonomy to sell Extreme Programming to upper management and pilot the AMA's first Extreme Programming project. Thank you, John and Doug, for allowing an inexperienced but enthusiastic programmer like me to try out my ideas and make some waves in your organization.

If I had to point to one person who has had the biggest impact on me and my journey, it would be Wyatt Sutherland. I met Wyatt in 2002 at ChAD, the Chicago Agile Developers group, back when he was the group's leader. I approached Wyatt about being his "apprentice" and he agreed to meet with me periodically for lunches and breakfasts. He did this despite his incredibly busy schedule as a traveling Agile consultant, music director at a local university, and father of four. Thank you, Wyatt, for your guidance during those years. It was a priceless gift and gave me the confidence to leave the AMA and aspire to work at companies like Object Mentor and ThoughtWorks.

I also need to thank my former employer, ThoughtWorks, for giving me access to a large group of people interested in contributing to this book, in particular my coauthor Adewale Oshineye. Thank you to ThoughtWorks' Chief Scientist, Martin Fowler, for spending some time with me and sharing your insights on the writing process. ThoughtWorks graciously paid for my travel when Obie Fernandez invited me to come speak about the Apprenticeship Patterns at Agile Atlanta in 2005. Thank you, Obie, for your friendship and encouragement during our project together in Auburn Hills, for the invitation to Agile Atlanta, and for letting me sleep at your place when I missed my flight home. :) Thank you to my friend Laurent Bossavit, who presented the patterns to XP France in 2005 and translated the transcript to English for me. Thank you to Daragh Farrell, for presenting the patterns at Geeknight Sydney in 2005 and sending me the video of the discussion. Thank you to Linda Rising, for inviting both me and Ade to PLoP 2005, where we received a bunch of important feedback and had our first (and so far only) opportunity to meet face-to-face (and another thanks to ThoughtWorks for flying Ade to Chicago from London to attend PLoP).

At the beginning of my research into these patterns, I reached out to a number of well-known people in the software development community. These people spent time with me on the phone, via email, or both, offering feedback and wisdom based on their decades of experience. I am grateful to Ken Auer, Jerry Weinberg, Norm Kerth, Ron Jeffries, Linda Rising, Dave Astels, and Pete McBreen for spending some of their precious time guiding me in my writing. At the same time, I (and later Ade) reached out to dozens of less-experienced people (like myself) to ask for their input on the patterns and to mine their stories for common themes.

Much thanks to Adam Williams, Chris McMahon, Daragh Farrell, Desi McAdam, Elizabeth Keogh, Emerson Clarke, Jake Scruggs, Kragen Sitaker, Ivan Moore, Joe Walnes, Jonathan Weiss, Kent Schnaith, Marten Gustafson, Matt Savage, Micah Martin, Michael Hale, Michelle Pace, Patrick Kua, Patrick Morrison, Ravi Mohan, Steven Baker, Steve Tooke, Tim Bacon, Paul Pagel, Enrique Comba Riepenhausen, Nuno Marques, Steve Smith, Daniel Sebban, Brian Brazil, Matthew Russell, Russ Miles, and Raph Cohn for corresponding with us and relating their ideas and stories for us to use.

In 2008 we launched *http://apprenticeship.oreilly.com*, where we posted the content of the patterns for feedback from the community. Thanks to everyone who contributed, including Julie Baumler, Bob Beany, Antony Marcano, Ken McNamara, Tom Novotny, Vikki Read, Michael Rolf, Joseph Taylor, and especially Michael Hunger, who was an active participant in the forums and provided us excellent feedback from his several manuscript reviews.

I also need to express my gratitude to the daily passengers of the Metra Union Pacific West Line train that runs from Chicago's Loop to the western suburbs. The majority of this book was written in the library-like silence of this train. Thank you for keeping to yourselves and enjoying your own books while I was writing mine. See you tomorrow!

I joined Obtiva in 2006, when Kevin Taylor convinced me that I should become its fourth employee rather than a subcontractor. It was certainly good advice, and has paid off in countless ways. I need to thank Kevin for supporting my untested ideas, handing me part of the company, cleaning up my continual messes, and taking care of so many unglamorous yet vital aspects of the business. I am excited about what the future holds for our company. One of the untested ideas that Kevin allowed me to run with was launching Obtiva's Software Studio and bringing on apprentices who we could nurture into senior developers. Since starting the Studio in April 2007 we have brought on six apprentices, and I need to express my sincere thankfulness to our first three apprentices, Brian Tatnall, Joseph Leddy, and Nate Jackson, who bore the brunt of my many shortcomings and inexperience. The trial and error that these guys endured has helped us gradually improve the apprenticeships of our most recent three apprentices, Colin Harris, Leah Welty-Rieger, and Turner King. Thanks to all six of you for your dedication, enthusiasm, and desire to learn and grow in often less-than-ideal circumstances.

Mary Treseler is the person responsible for encouraging us to publish this project. From the first time she read our initial patterns in 2005, she found that they resonated with her, despite the fact that she was not a programmer herself. Thank you, Mary, for hearing our intent despite our inexperience as writers, and for sticking with us patiently through the years.

I was blessed with growing up in a very stable family. Although we moved around a lot, my mom and dad were steadfast in their examples as parents, spouses, and Christians. Having them as role models has made my transition into adulthood, marriage, and parenthood relatively painless. Marcia Hoover and Rick Hoover were a constant source of encouragement for me as a writer, from a very early age. Thank you, Mom and Dad, for nurturing my writing instincts.

Although I didn't start programming until I was 26, I didn't waste any time starting a family: my daughter was born when I was 24, just a few months before finishing graduate school. While starting a family under those circumstances is incredibly challenging, one of the things that my children gave me as a father was a laser focus on my responsibilities. There hasn't been a day since Rose's birth in 1999 when I could afford to be unemployed, and that is incredibly motivating for someone starting a new career. As my children have grown from babies to elementary-age kids, I have been inspired by watching them overcome obstacles in their own learning processes. This has reminded me to continue my own lifelong learning and to pursue knowledge as tenaciously as they do. Rose, Ricky, and Charlie, thank you for loving me unconditionally and for putting up with your fourth sibling, Daddy's laptop. You should be seeing a bit less of it in the future now that this book is finished.

Ade's Acknowledgments

First of all I'd like to thank all the people that Dave thanked. Without them Dave wouldn't be here and therefore neither would I.

I'd like to thank the Pragmatic Programmers (Andy and Dave for the inspiration that introduced me to the C2 wiki and the Extreme Tuesday Club. Without those influences I wouldn't have found Laurent Bossavit's Bookshelved wiki, and I wouldn't have known who Dave was when he joined ThoughtWorks.

Of course, I wouldn't have been a consultant there if, at an XTC evening at the Old Bank of England, Paul Hammant hadn't challenged me to justify my unwillingness to join ThoughtWorks. Thanks, Paul. Being at TW opened a lot of doors. For example, the sponsorship of ThoughtWorks' erstwhile Innovation Director, Dave Farley, meant I could go to Allerton for the PLoP conference and meet Dave in person.

The people who gave up their time to be quizzed about the details of their careers for this book know who they are. I can't name you all here, but you have my eternal gratitude. The same applies to our reviewers. Thank you for taking the time to show us how to make this a better book.

Ravi Mohan didn't just share his experiences with us. He asked us hard questions about every aspect of the book and the concept of software craftsmanship. His willingness to do the background reading, to change his mind, and to keep asking for definitions kept us honest. Thanks, Ravi.

I'd also like to thank Robert Konigsberg and Eve Andersson for providing incredibly detailed feedback on early versions of the manuscript.

I'd like to thank Enrique Comba Riepenhausen for creating the initial OmniGraffle diagrams. Without his help, you would be looking at some fairly ugly autogenerated diagrams made using Graphviz.

Writing a book on apprenticeship would have been impossible without a mentor. Ivan Moore didn't stop being my mentor just because we didn't work together anymore. I'll always be grateful for that, as well as the tea.

I'd also like to thank Mary Treseler for taking a chance on Dave and me despite all the missed deadlines. We owe you one.

Finally, I'd like to thank my parents. They bought me my first computers, and they realized that I should be a professional programmer many years before I did. If I'd listened to them when I was younger, my path would have been shorter and more straightforward.

SOFTWARE CRAFTSMANSHIP MANIFESTO

NOTE

In March 2009, after prolonged discussion on the software_craftsmanship mailing list, the following manifesto was drafted.

As aspiring Software Craftsmen we are raising the bar of professional software development by practicing it and helping others learn the craft. Through this work we have come to value:

Not only working software, but also well-crafted software

Not only responding to change, but also steadily adding value

Not only individuals and interactions, but also a community of professionals

Not only customer collaboration, but also productive partnerships

That is, in pursuit of the items on the left, we have found the items on the right to be indispensable.

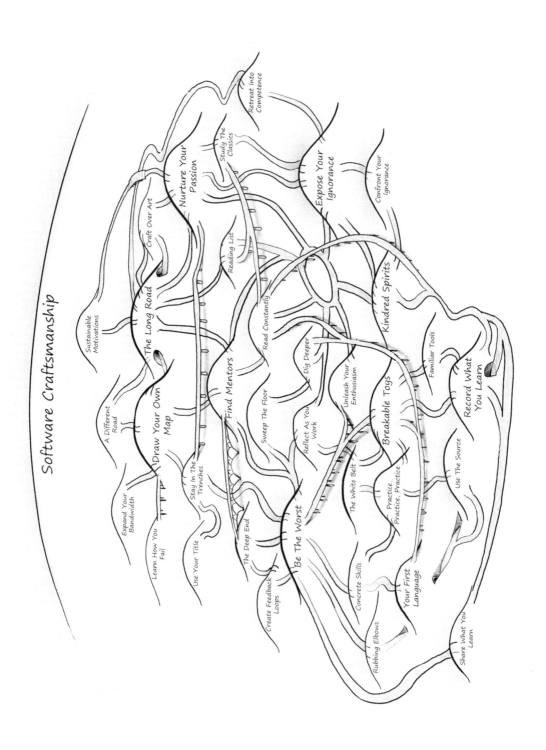

Software Craftsmanship

CHAPTER ONE

Introduction

**Apprenticeship makes a difference because it instills a
lifelong passion to master the craft. It instills a passion
for perpetual learning and, in the process, enables the
apprentice to become a great developer.**

—Pete McBreen, Software Craftsmanship

This book is written for software apprentices—for people who have had a taste of developing
software and want to take it further, but need some guidance. Whether you have a college
degree from a prestigious computer science program or are entirely self-taught, you recognize
that there are great developers out there, and you aspire to achieve the same mastery that they
possess. This book is written entirely for you—not for your boss, not for your team leader, not
for your professor. There are many other books we would recommend for people in those roles,
but this book is for people at the beginning of the journey.

While writing this book, we were heavily influenced by the principles and ideals of software
craftsmanship. Indeed, the title of the book reflects this. The concept of apprenticeship is based
on the medieval craft model, where small teams of practitioners work together and
inexperienced apprentices help the journeymen and master craftsmen do their work. One of
our goals for this book is to inspire the people who love to create software to stay focused on
their craft. The journey discussed here starts with "Hello world!", but where does it end? Far
too often, it ends with a promotion to middle management. Too many talented people
thoughtlessly take that promotion and find themselves just a few years later in jobs they don't
enjoy and yearning for retirement. But for those who have a knack for developing software
and enjoy the learning process, software development is a career that can last a lifetime, and
it can be a great ride.

But before that ride can begin, we're going to tell you Dave's story and provide some
definitions. His story shows one way that apprenticeship patterns can be combined to create
powerful forces in your personal growth as a software developer. On the other hand, the

definitions are an attempt to gather in one place the set of ideas that underpin software craftsmanship, and to answer some common questions about these ideas.

Dave's story (told with a sprinkling of apprenticeship patterns)

My first language was Perl, but that was only after two previous failed attempts at learning how to program. When I was 12, I tried to teach myself BASIC on my Apple IIe after watching the movie *Tron* and being inspired by the idea of an entire world existing inside my computer. I bought a BASIC manual published by Apple, but I couldn't figure out how to do anything compelling with the language. When I realized I wasn't going to be able to build anything other than text-based games, I eventually gave up. Then when I was 25, I tried to teach myself Java by reading a *Dummies* book and slowly working through the exercises, creating Java applets. I ended up truly feeling like a dummy, and gave up because everything seemed so difficult. It wasn't until I was 26 and found two mentors that my first language finally stuck. I found these mentors at Edventions LLC in Skokie, Illinois, at the height of the dot-com bubble. Irv Shapiro, the founder of the company, knew that I wanted to become a programmer (he had hired me as an online content editor) and needed me to learn Perl. He plopped *Programming Perl* (*http://oreilly .com/catalog/9780596000271/*) down on my desk and described a breakable toy that I could build as a learning exercise. Over the next few days, I consumed *Programming Perl*, though it was a pretty heavy-duty book for a newbie like me. So I followed it up with a book from my reading list, a more digestible Visual QuickStart Guide. My other mentor was Steve Bunes, the CTO of Edventions, who sat down and rubbed elbows with me periodically, showing me some powerful debugging techniques that I still use today. The toughest pattern to apply on the way to completing the first version of the breakable toy was exposing my ignorance to the experienced Perl programmers and system administrators in the nearby developers' workspace. But it was worth swallowing my pride because they gave me a few quick pointers on shebangs and Unix file permissions, which allowed me to quickly finish the breakable toy and knock Irv and Steve's socks off.

Two years later I was looking for opportunities to move my career beyond my beloved (but increasingly unappreciated) Perl and pick up some new skills. I expanded my bandwidth by diving into extreme programming (XP) and agile development, which were at the height of their hype cycle at that time. I spent a few days at the nearby XP/Agile Universe conference, drinking from that firehose of new information. Meeting and listening to people like Ron Jeffries, Martin Fowler, "Uncle" Bob Martin, Alistair Cockburn, and Kent Beck was an overwhelming experience, and I emerged from the conference as an official object-oriented, extreme programming wannabe. I discovered that Joshua Kerievsky was working on *Refactoring to Patterns* which sounded impressive, so I found a kindred spirit to study it with me. We soon discovered that we were getting ahead of ourselves, since I didn't know what refactoring or patterns even meant. So I looked for books that were more appropriate for my experience level. This ultimately led me to *Object-Oriented Software Construction* and *A Pattern Language*. I still wanted to get back to *Refactoring to Patterns* later, so I added it to my reading list.

I started learning Ruby in 2002 with that same kindred spirit, but I was unable to find many ways of using it in my day job until Ruby on Rails (*http://rubyonrails.org*) came on the scene. In 2005 I picked up Ruby again in an effort to find ways to work with it on a day-to-day basis. I was building a breakable toy with it, but found myself thinking too much like a Perl programmer. For any programmer proficient in his first language, it's always a temptation to fall back to the standards and idioms of your native language when you're learning a new language. Ruby has a reputation for elegance and simplicity, and the code I was writing felt ugly and awkward, so I figured I was doing something wrong. I made the conscious decision to wear the white belt, so I set aside my Perl expertise and dug into the Ruby documentation. Soon thereafter, I found what I needed and refactored my convoluted code into a nice, standard method call (String#scan, for you curious Rubyists out there). To help keep all this new information stuck in my head, I decided to expose my ignorance by recording what I had learned on my website for all to see.*

What Is Software Craftsmanship?

The dictionary definitions for simple words like craft, craftsmanship, apprentice, journeyman, and master are insufficient for our needs in this book. They are often circular (with craft being defined in terms of the skill a craftsman possesses, a craftsman being defined as someone who exhibits craftsmanship, and craftsmanship being defined as the quality that binds together the craftsmen working in the craft tradition), seldom grounded in the history of the guild system in specific countries, and often generalized to describe anything that is skillfully constructed. In short, these definitions fail to exclude anything and so include everything. We need more than that.

Google lists 61,800 references to the phrase "software craftsmanship,"† but few of those references offer usable definitions to someone looking for career guidance. Sadly, many of the articles are written by well-meaning programmers who have found that there is something useful hidden away in this tangle of related concepts, but are unable to meaningfully extract it.

Pete McBreen's book *Software Craftsmanship* is an attempt to put together a manifesto for an alternative approach to software development, aimed at those who do not operate under the assumption that software development is an engineering discipline or a science. But even McBreen's inspiring work is flawed. It does not distinguish between software craftsmanship as practiced today, and software craftsmanship as he would like it to be practiced. Nor does he make a clear enough distinction between his vision and medieval notions of crafts as highly skilled industries overseen by secretive guilds. He makes the mistake of defining software craftsmanship in opposition to software engineering, and asking his readers to choose between them. We think that a craft model can be defined in a positive way that doesn't exclude those

---

* *http://redsquirrel.com/cgi-bin/dave/craftsmanship/ruby.white.belt.html*

† *http://www.google.co.uk/search?q=%22software+craftsmanship%22*

people who feel that there's something valuable in the attempt to build a discipline of software engineering.

The model that we draw inspiration from was prevalent in medieval Europe until the start of the Industrial Revolution (*The Craftsman*, pp. 52–80). In that model, the guilds controlled the masters and the masters controlled those who worked and lived in their workshops. The masters owned the workshops and had absolute authority. Below them in this strict hierarchy were the journeymen. They were usually craftsmen who had yet to achieve their *chef d'oeuvre élève* or "high masterpiece" that would demonstrate they were sufficiently skilled to be considered masters.

The journeymen were nomadic, and were the only means by which new techniques could pass from city to city. As well as bringing in new techniques, journeymen would supervise the day-to-day activities of the apprentices. The apprentices would work for one master for several years until they graduated to the ranks of journeymen by proving they had absorbed the basic skills and values of their craft. A person who did not fit into the guild's hierarchy could not legally practice his craft.

As you can imagine, this system was open to abuse and is impractical, if not illegal, in today's world. We do not wish to repeat the mistakes that moved this model to the margins of modern society. Instead, we believe it is possible to reject the romantic fantasy of the craftsman's workshop in favor of a modern craft studio where we are free to improve upon the past, not just imitate it.

One of the lessons we've learned from the Agile development movement is that just telling people to do things doesn't create lasting or sustainable change. When the people you've advised encounter a situation that isn't covered by the rules, they're lost. However, if those same people have imbibed the *values* that underpin the rules, they can come up with new rules to fit any situation. Our goal here is not simply to hand people a rule book, but to give them the ability to create new practices for new contexts, which in turn drives the discipline of software development forward.

Our vision of software craftsmanship is partly a distillation of the values of the highly skilled individuals we've interviewed for this book, and partly an expression of the kind of community we would like to see emerge. The ideas in this book are a starting point for that vision. So when we use the phrase *software craftsmanship* we're talking about a community of practice united and defined by overlapping values, including:

- An attachment to Carol Dweck's research, which calls for a "growth mindset." This entails a belief that you can be better and everything can be improved if you're prepared to work at it. In her words, "effort is what *makes* you smart or talented" (*Mindset*, p. 16), and failure is merely an incentive to try a different approach next time. It is the opposite of the belief that we're all born with a given amount of talent, and that failure is an indication that you don't have enough of it.

- A need to always be adapting and changing based on the feedback you get from the world around you. Atul Gawande refers to this as a willingness to "recognize the inadequacies in what you do and to seek out solutions" (*Better*, p. 257).

- A desire to be pragmatic rather than dogmatic. This involves a willingness to trade off theoretical purity or future perfection in favor of getting things done today.

- A belief that it is better to share what we know than to create scarcity by hoarding it. This is often connected to an involvement in the Free and Open Source Software communities.

- A willingness to experiment and be proven wrong. This means we try stuff. We fail. Then we use the lessons from that failure in the next experiment. As Virginia Postrel puts it: "not every experiment or idea is a good one, but only by trying new ideas do we discover genuine improvements. And there is always more to be done. Every improvement can be improved still further; every new idea makes still more new combinations possible" (*Future Enemies*, p. 59).

- A dedication to what psychologists call an internal locus of control.[‡] This involves taking control of and responsibility for our destinies rather than just waiting for someone else to give us the answers.

- A focus on individuals rather than groups. This is not a movement with leaders and followers. Instead, we are a group of people who want to improve our skills and have discovered that debate, dissent, and disagreement rather than blind deference to self-proclaimed authority are the way to get there. We believe that we are all on the same journey and that the change we seek is in ourselves, not the world. This is why this book doesn't focus on how to fix your team, but rather on ways to improve your own skills.

- A commitment to inclusiveness. We don't reject enterprise software development, or computer science or software engineering (in fact, Ade has the word "engineer" in his current job title). Instead, we think that a useful system should be able to identify and absorb the best ideas from all elements of the software development community.

- We are skill-centric rather than process-centric. For us, it is more important to be highly skilled than to be using the "right" process. This idea has consequences. Gawande asked, "Is medicine a craft or an industry? If medicine is a craft, then you focus on teaching obstetricians to acquire a set of artisanal skills.... You do research to find new techniques. You accept that things will not always work out in everyone's hands" (*Better*, p. 192). This idea suggests that no process or tool is going to make everyone equally successful. Even though we can all improve, there will always be discrepancies in our skill levels.

- A strong preference for what Etienne Wenger calls "situated learning."[§] This is an idea that the software community has tried to capture with patterns like Expert in Earshot.[‖] Its

‡ *http://en.wikipedia.org/wiki/Locus_of_control*

§ *http://c2.com/cgi/wiki?LegitimatePeripheralParticipation*

‖ *http://c2.com/cgi/wiki?ExpertInEarshot*

essence is that the best way to learn is to be in the same room with people who are trying to achieve some goal using the skills you wish to learn.

This value system gives rise to different roles with different responsibilities, as discussed in the following sections.

What Does It Mean to Be an Apprentice?

When discussing what it means to be an apprentice, Marten Gustafson, one of our interviewees, put it best when he said, "I guess it basically means having the attitude that there's always a better/smarter/faster way to do what you just did and what you're currently doing. Apprenticeship is the state/process of evolving and looking for better ways and finding people, companies and situations that force you to learn those better/smarter/faster ways." We think there's a lot of value in having this internal drive that is not dependent on anyone else to bestow solutions upon you, and that leads you to find constructive ways of dealing with problems. As Dweck writes, "It is not an internal quantity that is fed by easy successes and diminished by failures.... It is not something we *give* to people by telling them about their high intelligence. It is something we equip them to get for themselves—by teaching them to value learning over the appearance of smartness, to relish challenge and to use errors as routes to mastery" (*Self-theories*, p. 4).

While the ideal situation would have you in a small team of fellow apprentices, journeymen, and a master, our understanding of apprenticeship does not require this arrangement. Your apprenticeship is under your control, and ultimately the outcome of your apprenticeship is your responsibility. While the course and progress of your apprenticeship are determined by you, the availability and quality of your mentors will also have a lasting impact on your craftsmanship.

Apprenticeship is the beginning of your journey as a software craftsman. During this time you will be primarily focused inward, intent on growing your craftsmanship. While you will benefit from the attention of your peers and more experienced developers, you must learn to grow yourself, to learn how you learn. This focus on yourself and your need to grow is the essence of what it means to be an apprentice.

An apprentice will eventually graduate from a position of few responsibilities beyond continuous learning to a position with wider and more outward-looking responsibilities, and we tend to believe that this transition is something that can only be seen in retrospect. At some point, an apprentice is approached by a master or a journeyman and told that her work and her role in the community are that of a journeyman. In such a case, the apprentice had previously begun taking on more responsibilities, and like a "boiled frog" had made a gradual but not discrete transition from one state to another. That transition may take longer for some people than for others. For some, the transition may take longer than their professional careers.

What Does It Mean to Be a Journeyman?

As you progress through the stages of craftsmanship, you retain the attributes of the previous stages. Therefore, like the apprentice, the journeyman and the master will maintain an inward focus in order to learn and grow in their craft. And yet, another focus is added for the journeyman. This new focus is on the connections between practitioners, the communication channels within and outside the team. Traditionally, a journeyman would move from master to master, along the way disseminating ideas between the various teams. The reality of modern software development is that you may be with a single team for a significantly long time; in this situation, you would focus on improving the connections within the one team. This focus will eventually expand into a responsibility to mentor those around you and to communicate with the rest of the industry.

The journeyman is focused on building an ever-larger portfolio of applications that demonstrates his progress in the craft; he moves between projects and masters, seeking to diversify and deepen his portfolio; he seeks to elevate his status within the community; and he strives to become ready to be a master.

The journeyman's responsibilities are wider than those of an apprentice. As such his failures can do more harm. Some of the patterns we will discuss are not appropriate for a journeyman, precisely because he has a greater responsibility to others who may see him as a mentor.

What Does It Mean to Be a Master?

Mastery involves performing all the roles of an apprentice or a journeyman as well as focusing on moving the industry forward. The "acquisition of consummate skill and technique" (*The Creative Habit*, p. 167) is just the start. Mastery involves taking that skill and turning it into a magnifying glass that can enhance the skills of others by orders of magnitude. This may take the form of creating new tools that cut through to the essence of software development, or it may involve training a generation of journeymen whose skills equal and then surpass your own. Or it may take the shape of something that we can't yet imagine. In short, masters view the acquisition, usage, and sharing of superior skill as the most important part of being a software craftsman.

The definitions of apprentice, journeyman, and master discussed here are not the kind you would find in any dictionary. This is something new. But we believe that the values inherent in our vision of software craftsmanship will help you to be as successful as you desire, whether you ultimately embrace them, enhance them, reject them, or follow a different road entirely.

What Is Apprenticeship?

The fundamental learning situation is one in which a person learns by helping someone who really knows what he is doing.

—Christopher Alexander et al., *A Pattern Language*, p. 413

The clichéd image of apprenticeship popularized by many books, including the 1945 edition of *Fifteen Craftsmen On Their Crafts* (p. 69) is that of a teenage boy with soot all over his face, working in a blacksmith's shop. The blacksmith, a gruff, experienced craftsman, forges his projects with the boy's assistance. Sometimes the boy is actively participating in the process; sometimes he is cleaning up the shop, yet still keeping a watchful eye on the master at work. Stereotypically, the boy's apprenticeship would last a few years, and other than knowledge, experience, food, and lodging, the boy would receive little else in the way of payment. Eventually, the boy would acquire enough skill to take on projects of his own, perhaps even leaving his first master to take on a role with more responsibility in a different shop. When the boy's apprenticeship was over, he could earn a living as a blacksmith, relying on his skills to provide shelter and food and tools for himself. In the modern world, an apprenticeship involving an accomplished software developer and a newcomer likely bears little resemblance to this stereotypical apprenticeship. So what's our current understanding of apprenticeship, and how does it transcend the cliché?

To be clear, in this book we are not attempting to describe our proposed ideal apprenticeship for a newcomer to software development. If we were writing for team leaders and project managers, then providing instructions to build the ideal apprenticeship would make sense, because these people actually have the power to facilitate that sort of experience. But this book is for newcomers to software development, the people in the trenches trying to figure out how to learn what they need to know in order to accomplish objectives such as getting a (better) job, completing their project, or becoming a great developer. Since most newcomers' experiences do not resemble the "ideal" apprenticeship, the modern concept of apprenticeship is mainly a frame of mind: you recognize that you are still at the beginning, even if you've been programming for several years, and you are prepared to take steps to create your apprenticeship out of the circumstances you are in.

Most people won't have an opportunity to work in a formal apprenticeship where they are being mentored by software craftsmen. In reality, most people have to claw and scratch their apprenticeships out of less-than-ideal situations. They might be facing overbearing and/or incompetent managers, de-motivated coworkers, impossible deadlines, and work environments that treat novice developers like workhorses, storing them in small, rectangular stalls with a PC and a crippled Internet connection. All of the lessons of this book are taken from the experiences of people (like us) who had to overcome these sorts of circumstances in order to reach the next level. Until our industry can heed the following advice of Pete McBreen, newcomers will continue to need books like this to help them create their own opportunities for learning.

> We can take the time needed to nurture apprentice developers because we are faced with the problem of abundance, rather than scarcity.... Today we have more developers than needed, but we have a shortage of *good* developers.
>
> —Pete McBreen, *Software Craftsmanship*, p. 93

Apprenticeship is a way to learn about being a professional software developer. Specifically, it is a way to learn to be like the most skilled software developers you can find. It involves seeking out good teachers, and taking opportunities to learn by working alongside them. It is the first step on the road toward becoming a different kind of software professional—one who wants to be more than just competent.

What Is an Apprenticeship Pattern?

An apprenticeship pattern attempts to offer guidance to someone working with the craft model on the ways in which they can improve the progress of their career. All our patterns have been extracted from our own experiences and those of the people we have interviewed. Like any good collection of patterns, they should strike you as unoriginal precisely because the people around you are already using them. The other quality that these patterns share is that of generativity. Every time you apply them you should get different results, and if they're used in the appropriate contexts they should improve your working environment. These are not algorithms that guarantee the same results on every execution. Instead they are tools that solve one set of problems and create new ones. The trick is to use your judgment to choose the problems you prefer.

This book is organized as a pattern language. A pattern language is an interconnected set of solutions to common problems in a specific domain. The original pattern language was written by Christopher Alexander in *A Pattern Language*, where he described over 250 patterns for designing everything from kitchens to houses to cities and even societies. Ward Cunningham and Kent Beck introduced pattern languages to the software industry in the 1990s, resulting in countless articles, books, and even conferences focused on design patterns. The best-known example of software design patterns literature is *Design Patterns* by "The Gang of Four" though Martin Fowler's *Refactoring* is a better example of a pattern *language*. To be clear, the book you're reading is not a book about designing software. Rather, it is a book about designing the beginning of your career in software development and setting yourself up to become great at what you do.

Where Did the Patterns Come From?

One of the principles of good software framework design is to extract the framework from a working system. Similarly, software design patterns are extracted from many working systems that have used the same solution to solve similar problems. This book was originally extracted from the stories of Dave's apprenticeship experiences, then tested and supplemented with

Ade's stories, and finally tested against the experiences of about 30 practitioners with experience levels ranging from a couple of years to many decades. We interviewed these people in order to test whether these patterns were actually common solutions to common problems, along with mining for other patterns that we hadn't recognized yet. We also participated in several workshops (PLoP 2005, Agile Atlanta meeting, and internal ThoughtWorks meetings) to help us focus on improving the structure and rigor of what we believed to be apprenticeship patterns. Finally, we have made much of this material freely available online in order to solicit feedback from the community.

Where Do We Go from Here?

As you begin learning about the patterns themselves, remember you have the power to choose them, combine them, and adapt them to your unique situation in an infinite number of ways. Understand that these patterns are written for a specific audience within a specific context. In the years ahead, some of the patterns will suddenly become relevant to you, and then just as suddenly some may feel inappropriate. An apprenticeship is a season in your career when your focus is more on your own growth than almost anything else. This is a time for you to delay your ambitions of immediately maximizing your earning potential in order to maximize your learning opportunities. Because of this, it is a season that affords a certain amount of selfishness. And once that season is over, your priorities will need to adapt. You will no longer be an apprentice, despite the fact that you still have much to learn, and your priorities will need to shift toward others: your customers, your colleagues, and your community.

CHAPTER TWO

Emptying the Cup

Can't you see the cup is already full and overflowing?

—The young philosopher

A Zen master of great renown was visited by a young philosopher who had traveled from a distant land to meet him. The master agreed to see him because the philosopher came with high recommendations by his teachers. The two sat under a tree to converse and the subject hastily turned to what the master could teach the young philosopher. Recognizing the flame of youth, the master smiled warmly and started to describe his meditation techniques. He was cut short by the philosopher, who said: "Yes, I understand what you are talking about! We did a similar technique at the temple, but instead we used images to focus!"

Once the philosopher was done explaining to the master how he was taught and practiced his meditation, the master spoke again. This time he tried to tell the young man about how one should be attuned to nature and the universe. He didn't get two sentences in when the philosopher cut him short again and started talking about how he had been taught meditation and so on and so on.

Once again, the master patiently waited for the young philosopher to end his excited explanations. When the philosopher was quiet again, the master spoke of seeing humor in every situation. The young man didn't lose any time and started to talk about his favorite jokes and how he thought they could relate to situations he had faced.

Once the philosopher was done, the Zen master invited him inside for a tea ceremony. The philosopher accepted gladly, having heard of how the master performed the ceremony like no other. Such a moment was always a privileged one with such a man. Once inside, the master performed flawlessly up to the point where he started to pour the tea in the cup. As the master was pouring, the philosopher noticed that the cup was being filled more than usual. The master kept pouring tea and the cup was soon full to the brim. Not knowing what to say, the young man stared at the master in astonishment. The master kept pouring as if nothing was wrong, and the cup started to overflow, spilling hot tea on the floor mattresses and the master's hakama. Not believing what he was seeing, the philosopher finally exclaimed: "Stop pouring! Can't you see the cup is already full and overflowing?"

With those words, the master gently placed the teapot back on the fire and looked at the young philosopher with his ever-present warm smile and said: "If you come to me with a cup that is already full, how can you expect me to give you something to drink?"

This story was adapted from Michel Grandmont's "Tasting a New Cup of Tea."* We retell it here to illustrate the sort of attitude a successful apprenticeship requires. The more experience you already have, the more effort you will need to put into "emptying your cup," clearing your mind of bad habits, setting aside the pride you have in your skills, and opening yourself up to the different, often counterintuitive, approaches of your more experienced colleagues.

The patterns in this chapter should provide you with the tools to start your apprenticeship on the right foot and with an open mind. Wearing The White Belt represents maintaining a beginner's mind regardless of your expertise. Unleashing Your Enthusiasm will propel you

---

* http://www.ironmag.com/archive/ironmag/2000_mg_reality_of_learning.htm

through common beginner roadblocks such as frustration, confusion, and discouragement and will allow you to venture deep into Your First Language. Acquiring Concrete Skills in a specific technology will open doors for you and give you opportunities to explore the more advanced patterns in later chapters. But don't allow yourself to become too comfortable! Use the final four patterns together to systematically acquire an increasingly broad set of technologies. Allow yourself to Expose Your Ignorance in a specific technology in order to focus your attention on what you need to learn next. Then Confront Your Ignorance and let your team and your customers watch you flex your knowledge-acquisition muscles. Eventually you'll have the opportunity to take on an audacious task, a chance to dive into The Deep End and either learn how to swim or sink to the bottom. That may sound scary, but there is no better time in your career to take this sort of risk. When all of this new information and mind-stretching becomes overwhelming, it's important to Retreat into Competence, remember how far you've come and the skills you've developed, and gather yourself to ascend to the next plateau.

Your First Language

> **By relieving the brain of all unnecessary work, a good
> notation sets it free to concentrate on more advanced
> problems, and in effect increases the mental power of the
> race.[...T]he technical terms of any profession or trade are
> incomprehensible to those who have never been trained
> to use them. But this is not because they are difficult in
> themselves. On the contrary they have invariably been
> introduced to make things easy.**
>
> *—Alfred North Whitehead, An Introduction to Mathematics*

Context

You are just starting out and have only a shallow understanding of one or two programming languages.

Problem

You feel your job depends on you delivering a solution written in a specific programming language and of the same standard of quality as your teammates. Alternatively, obtaining a job in the first place depends on your proficiency in a specific programming language.

Solution

Pick a language. Become fluent in it. For the next few years this will be the main language you use to solve problems, as well as the default skill you hone whenever you are practicing. Making this choice is a challenge. It is important that you carefully weigh the options, as this is the foundation upon which your early career will be built.

If you are asked to solve a problem and it dictates a programming language, let the drive toward the solution direct your learning. If you're pursuing a job that requires a specific language, build a toy application using that language, preferably an open source project so it is easy for your prospective employer to see a sample of your work. Either way, ask the most experienced and available programmer you know for ongoing help. Having someone immediately available can be the difference between a problem taking minutes or days of your time. However, keep in mind that you don't want to become completely dependent on your more experienced friend to solve all your problems.

One of the fundamental ways to improve the experience of learning your first language is to have an actual problem to solve. This helps to ground your learning in reality and provides you with your first, relatively large, feedback loop. Learning with the small, contrived examples in books and articles is limiting, and you lose the benefit of applying your discoveries to a problem you have in your head, which, after all, is what you'd be doing on the job. The fundamental way to improve this experience is to seek out opportunities to create feedback loops. In particular, creating short feedback loops helps you gauge your progress. Some languages have better tools for feedback than others, but regardless of the language, you can take some steps to set up a learning sandbox to experiment in.

In Ruby, there is the interactive command-line tool irb. In Rails, there is script/console. Similarly, Erlang has erb. Firebug provides many useful ways to explore the JavaScript runtime in the Firefox web browser, including an interactive shell. Many languages provide equivalent tools.

Sometimes these tools won't suffice and you'll need a bigger sandbox. Dave likes to keep an empty Java class open in his IDE when he needs to play around with an unfamiliar API or language feature:

```
public class Main {
    public static void main(String[] args) throws Exception {
        System.out.println(/*play with stuff here*/);
    }
}
```

Once you've learned enough to actually start writing code, test-driven development techniques can keep you focused on taking small steps and ensure you check your assumptions. Thanks to the popularity of test-driven development, you'll be hard-pressed to find a language that doesn't have a testing framework. Don't hesitate to write simple tests to check your understanding of the language, or just to familiarize yourself with the testing framework.

Start by taking almost insanely small steps; as you learn more, your steps can grow correspondingly larger. For instance, the Ruby language has a feature that lets you apply a block of code to every element in a list and collect the results into a new list. You might write the following code to clarify your understanding of this feature:

```
require "test/unit"

class LearningTest < Test::Unit::TestCase
    def test_my_understanding_of_blocks_and_procs
        original = [1, 2, 3]
        expected = [2, 3, 4]
        p = Proc.new { |n| n + 1 }
        assert_equal expected, original.map(&p)
    end
end
```

You're not limited to using learning tests for learning a language; you can also apply this process to learning about how other people's libraries work. Over time, these vendor tests (as Ade christened them during a lightning talk at the London Test Automation Conference[†]) can be used to check that upgrading to a later version of a library will not break your system. When the system breaks, the tests point to the new library as the source of the problem since the only functionality they exercise is that which you depend on the library to provide. In well-factored

---

† Ade Oshineye, "Testing Heresies." Available at: *http://www.youtube.com/watch?v=47nuBTRB51c#t=23m34s*.

systems, they can also be used to verify that a different implementation of a library's functionality does all the things you need.

Eventually, you will go from just writing learning tests to writing tests that check your actual code rather than your understanding of language constructs and APIs. Over time, you will find that there are many other techniques beyond simple unit testing that use the computer to verify your work as well as communicate with other members of your team.

The following is a discussion of learning to think differently by learning a new language, but the advice of Ralph Johnson (coauthor of *Design Patterns*) applies to a first language as well.

> *Question:* So assuming someone did want to learn to think differently, what would you go with? Ruby, Python, Smalltalk?
>
> *Answer:* I prefer Smalltalk. But it doesn't matter what I prefer. You should choose a language based on who is around you. Do you know somebody who is a fan of one of these languages? Could you talk regularly with this person? Better yet, could you do a project with this person?
>
> By far the best way to learn a language is to work with an expert in it. You should pick a language based on people who you know. One expert is all it takes, but you need one.
>
> The best situation is where you work regularly with the expert on a project using the language, even if it is only every Thursday night. It would be almost as good if you would work on the project on your own but bring code samples to the expert when you have lunch twice a week.
>
> It is possible to learn a language on your own, but it takes a long time to learn the spirit of a language unless you interact with experts.
>
> —Ralph Johnson on learning a language‡

Ralph's advice ties directly into the Find Mentors pattern and the impact that mentors can have on your learning. Thus, the availability of feedback from a nearby language expert should be a major factor when selecting your first language. We should also mention that by choosing a language, you're also opting into a virtual community of practice with established idioms, social gatherings, and mechanisms for communication. You should take advantage of that support network so that you don't just learn a language, but in fact join your first community of Kindred Spirits. The preferred work, boundaries, prejudices, and beliefs of this community will be all you have at first. When choosing to learn a language, you should attend meetings of a local group of that language's enthusiasts (or visit one of their Internet forums) and see if you want to belong to that community.

One of the advantages of belonging to a community that shares its code is that you learn to go beyond the obvious grammatical constructs and start to express yourself idiomatically. But that's just the beginning. Every language also has its own subtleties that are difficult to pick up solely by reading other people's code.

---

‡ *http://groups.yahoo.com/group/domaindrivendesign/message/2145*

For example, in XSLT there is the Muenchian method, while Perl has the Schwartzian Transform and C has Duff's Device. These techniques can all be learned by reading code, but learning to appreciate why they're important and when to use them requires the pooled experiences of a community. Sometimes this pool exists only as an oral tradition, and you have to talk to a particular person in order to gain the knowledge. Sometimes the knowledge exists only in the archives of a mailing list or perhaps in an online cookbook, where the lack of context makes it hard to appreciate its significance. In these situations, people new to the language have to immerse themselves in the community for years in order to tap into this pool of knowledge. Nowadays, though, these subtleties are often captured in books like *Effective Perl Programming* (Addison-Wesley), *Effective Java* (Prentice Hall), and *Effective C++* (Addison-Wesley). Reading books such as these as soon as you have mastered the basic syntax can greatly accelerate your learning and help you avoid common mistakes.

All this will help you dig deeper into your first language. For several years, your first language will be the framework against which you learn other languages. The better you know your first language, the easier it will be to learn your next language. Although you will primarily be using this language to solve day-to-day problems and deliver functionality, periodically take some time to stretch it beyond where you would in the normal course of your work. Stretching the language in unconventional directions will help you discover where one language excels and one language struggles.

Eric Merritt's blog post "The Shape of Your Mind" dives into how programming languages can have a profound impact on your problem-solving skills:

> [I]n many ways programming languages act quite a lot like the devices used to shape the skulls of infants in Paracas, the feet of Han women or the necks of Karen Paduang women. In the case of these languages, instead of shaping the skull they tend to shape the way we think about problems, the way we form ideas and the way those ideas are applied to a particular problem. For example, if you have only every written code in early versions of Fortran (Fortran 77 and before) then you probably don't even know recursion exists. Also, if you have only ever coded in Haskell you probably would know very little about imperative style loops.
>
> —Eric Merritt, "The Shape of Your Mind"[§]

One danger of digging deep into your first language is getting stuck. It likely will remain with you throughout your career as your native tongue. But do not allow your proficiency in it to prevent you from learning and using other languages. A healthy career should introduce you to the diverse language landscape of software development. Each language provides an opportunity to solve problems using different paradigms. As you move beyond your first language, look for opportunities to learn languages that take a radically different approach than the ones you already know. Apprentices comfortable with an object-oriented language should explore a functional programming language. Apprentices comfortable with dynamic typing should explore static typing. Apprentices comfortable with server-side programming should

§ *http://erlangish.blogspot.com/2007/05/shape-of-your-mind.html*

explore user interface design. Along the way, you will certainly develop preferences for languages and problem-solving approaches, but avoid the dogmatic, religious subcultures that try to push you toward a one-size-fits-all approach. This broadening is the first small step toward the wide-ranging mastery required of a master craftsman.

> You shouldn't be wedded to any particular technology, but have a broad enough background and experience base to allow you to choose good solutions in particular situations.
>
> —Dave Thomas and Andy Hunt, *The Pragmatic Programmer*, p. xviii

Action

Find your language's specification. Read it. For some languages this may be as easy as picking up a published book. For others there may only be a grammar available. For still others the only specification may exist in the language's implementation. Consider taking up the challenge of writing the specification.

If the language's standard library is open source, read through it using the techniques described in the Use the Source pattern. You may not be impressed by the quality of the code you see there, but keep in mind that the writers of that code had no community to learn from and had to make things up as they went. Consider sending them a patch to fix any bugs you spot.

Another approach you can take to building up your knowledge of a language is to ask the people you work with how they chose the first language they mastered. Then add the criteria they give you to the set you already used when you chose your first language. These will come in handy when it is time to choose your next language.

Finally, you can find out more about the idioms we mentioned earlier: the Muenchian method, the Schwartzian Transform, and Duff's Device. They're all named after programmers who had a practical problem to solve. Try to track down the problems that these idioms were originally meant to solve, and ask yourself how you would solve the same problems in your primary language.

See Also

"Breakable Toys" (page 79), "Dig Deeper" (page 105), "Find Mentors" (page 61), "The Long Road" (page 38), and "Use the Source" (page 82).

The White Belt

> As a rule, each step should have a feeling of entrance. This is beginner's mind—the state of *becoming*.
>
> —Shunryu Suzuki, *Zen Mind, Beginner's Mind*

Context

You have developed a deep understanding of your first language and are walking comfortably on a plateau of competence. Your colleagues recognize your abilities and call on you to help them solve problems in your area of expertise. You have pride in your skills.

Problem

You are struggling to learn new things and it seems somehow harder than it was before to acquire new skills. The pace of your self-education seems to be slowing down despite your best efforts. You fear that your personal development may have stalled.

Solution

While retaining the confidence you have gained through your learning, set your previous knowledge aside as you approach new situations. As Yoda so wisely says in *The Empire Strikes Back*, "You must unlearn what you have learned."

Wearing the white belt is based on the realization that while the black belt *knows* the way, the white belt has no choice but to *learn* the way.

Part of the approach Dave took as a family therapist included maintaining a *not knowing* stance. Families in difficult circumstances were experiencing a unique reality that, despite his training, Dave knew he could not fully appreciate. While he acknowledged his skills at facilitating constructive questions and conversations, Dave was taught to refrain from believing that he had any expert knowledge into the realities that these families experienced. While this may seem counterintuitive, in reality it fosters an attitude of respect and curiosity that opens up unforeseen possibilities and solutions. Rather than pushing solutions down on the family, Dave's *not knowing* stance helped him to collaborate with the family to find solutions as a team.

Taking this approach to learning new technologies accelerates the learning process tremendously. Training yourself to suspend the use of your customary programming idioms allows you to discover new possibilities. However, as a programmer finally feeling proud of achieving a significant level of expertise, taking a step toward ignorance and allowing yourself to look foolish can be painful. But consider the words of George Leonard from the final pages of *Mastery*:

> How many times have you failed to try something new out of fear of being thought silly? How often have you censored your spontaneity out of fear of being thought childish? ... Psychologist Abraham Maslow discovered a childlike quality in people who have met an unusually high degree of their potential. Ashleigh Montagu used the term neotany (from neonate, meaning newborn) to describe geniuses such as Mozart and Einstein. What we frown at as foolish in our friends, or ourselves, we're likely to smile at as merely eccentric in a world-renowned genius, never stopping to think that the freedom to be foolish might well be one of the keys to the genius's success.

Or take the following example of a 10-year industry veteran keeping an open mind and learning something new:

> I'd been writing software professionally and quite successfully for ten years and TDD for several years before I came across the unfortunately named "Working Effectively with Legacy Code" book by Michael Feathers, Prentice Hall. This book had an immediate and profound impact on how I write code, and I bought copies for all the other developers in my small company and required they read it. Since then, my codebase has gradually improved into a better tested, more loosely coupled, and more adaptable system that also happens to be a lot more fun to work with.
>
> —Steve Smith, email

As Steve learned, we have to be able to put aside our past experiences and preconceptions to allow new knowledge in. This is especially difficult when trying to learn your second programming language, because it is likely the first time that you have to sacrifice productivity in order to improve your skills. Previously you would have approached problems as empty cups, with few preconceptions about "the correct way" to solve them. Now you must try to avoid synthesizing new and old knowledge until the new knowledge has had time to sink in, and approach this new knowledge with the mind of a beginner. This may mean losing some productivity in the short term in order take a leap forward once you master the new approach.

> In order to climb, you must leave the sure footing, letting go of what you already do well and possibly slipping downward into a ravine. If you never let go of what you already do well, you may continue to make steady progress, but you'll never get off the plateau.
>
> —Jerry Weinberg, *Becoming a Technical Leader*, p. 42

One of the benefits of adopting this mindset when learning a new language, tool, or business domain is that you are open to learning how to express yourself idiomatically, thus smoothing your communication with the existing community. By avoiding the old problem of "writing Fortran in any language" you gain a far deeper understanding of the new knowledge. Thus, when you eventually reconcile new and old knowledge you are better placed to develop productive insights from both fields.

Take the following Java code as an example. It generates random numbers for the United Kingdom's National Lottery by printing a set of six distinct numbers from 1 to 49 inclusive:

```java
public class Lottery {
    private static final int NUMBER_OF_RANDOM_NUMBERS = 6;
    private static final int MAX_RANDOM_NUMBER = 49;

    public static void main(String[] args) {
        SortedSet randomNumbers = new TreeSet();
        Random random = new Random();
        while (randomNumbers.size() < NUMBER_OF_RANDOM_NUMBERS) {
            Integer randomNumber = new Integer(random.nextInt(MAX_RANDOM_NUMBER) + 1);
            randomNumbers.add(randomNumber);
        }
        System.out.println(randomNumbers);
```

```
        }
    }
```

If you were asked to reimplement this in a slightly different language like Io (which is designed to have a very minimal syntax while still being approachable to mainstream programmers), you could reuse a lot of your Java knowledge and write it like this:

```
list := List clone

while (list size < 6,
    n := Random value(1 50) floor
    list appendIfAbsent( n )
)

list sort print
```

But if you were asked to implement it in a radically different language like J, you would find this approach doesn't work. Only by "wearing the white belt"—accepting that in a language that doesn't have loops there must be a radically different but nonetheless valid way of solving problems—can you make progress. So in idiomatic J, the answer is:

```
sort 1 + (6 ? 49)
```

Later on we will show you patterns to help you practice, devise toy programs, and consciously reflect on the work you're doing. These patterns will allow you to appreciate the deeper commonalities between the different sets of knowledge that you possess, and create situations where you can hone your skills without the pressure to maintain your normal levels of productivity.

Action

Find an opportunity to unlearn something. Ideally, this would be something that forces you to put aside your previous experience.

For instance, take a program you have written in one programming paradigm (e.g., imperative, object-oriented, functional, array/vector-oriented, etc.) and implement it in a language that uses a different paradigm. Make sure your new implementation follows the idioms of the new language. If all the languages you know use the same paradigm (e.g., object orientation), then this is also an opportunity to learn a new paradigm.

This pattern goes beyond programming languages, but that happens to be one area where misconceptions can easily arise. So find someone who uses a programming language or a set of technologies that are unfamiliar to you. Ask that person to explain some of the misconceptions that people from your particular background usually have about their community.

See Also

"Breakable Toys" (page 79), "Practice, Practice, Practice" (page 77), and "Reflect As You Work" (page 85).

Unleash Your Enthusiasm

Craftsmen take on only eager apprentices who are willing to learn the craft of software development.

...

Apprentices are an essential part of software craftsmanship because they bring an enthusiasm and drive for learning that infect everyone else.

—*Pete McBreen, Software Craftsmanship*

Context

You have an insatiable excitement and curiosity regarding the craft of software development.

Problem

You find yourself holding back, conscious of how much more enthusiasm you have for the work than your colleagues do.

Solution

Despite (and because of!) your inexperience, you bring some unique attributes to your team, including an infectious enthusiasm. Do not allow anyone to dampen your excitement for the craft—it is a precious commodity and will accelerate your learning.

As a software developer, you will inevitably work as part of a team. In any group setting, there is a tendency to conform to the norm, particularly for newcomers. Most teams are not hyper-passionate or overly enthusiastic about technology. Predictably, they are focused on delivering the next project or improving on the aspects of the development life cycle that are causing them pain. Therefore, enthusiastic apprentices can often succumb to the urge to fly under the radar. They either repress their enthusiasm altogether, or allow it to manifest only outside of their day jobs.

There are certainly risks involved in unleashing your enthusiasm on an established team. If morale is low or if the team is not welcoming of newcomers, you will likely get some eye-rolling behind your back. You could certainly make a poor impression on people who value competence more than learning ability, particularly when you expose your ignorance. Like any pattern, this one should not be applied blindly. Team dynamics should always be considered. If you find yourself on a team that does not accept your excitement, you will need to find ways to nurture your passion.

However, on a team that is open to the excitement and contributions of an apprentice, you will provide some unique qualities that more experienced developers rely upon, such as unfettered imagination and enthusiasm. This is the time in your career when it makes the most sense to take risks and speak your mind. You have very little to lose. Your ideas and passions will add intelligence and diversity to your team. In James Surowiecki's *The Wisdom of Crowds*, he repeatedly points to diversity of thought as a key ingredient of collective intelligence.

An intriguing study on the collective mind of aircraft carrier crews showed that newcomers played an important role in the complex, coordinated group activities required to safely operate an enormous boat with fighter jets constantly coming and going. The researchers found that it is actually healthier for a team to consist of people with varying levels of experience.

> Comprehension can be increased if more levels of experience are connected, as when newcomers who take nothing for granted interrelate more often with old-timers who think they have seen it all.
>
> —Karl Weick and Karlene Roberts, "Collective Mind in Organizations," p. 366

Ultimately, unleashing your enthusiasm is one of the relatively few responsibilities of the apprentice. You may not bring deep knowledge or hyper-productivity, but it is your duty to inject some excitement into your team and question everything. You are in the unique (and temporary) position of having a fresh perspective, which should allow you to offer some useful suggestions for improvement.

> Craftsmen learn from the apprentices, even as the apprentices learn from them. Enthusiastic beginners not only renew the craftsmen, but also challenge the craftsmen by bringing in new ideas from the outside. A well chosen apprentice can make even a master craftsman more productive.
>
> —Pete McBreen, *Software Craftsmanship*, p. 75

Action

Think of the last time you had an idea but didn't propose it. Find the person you would have suggested it to and describe your idea to her. If she points out flaws, try to persuade her to help you improve it.

See Also

"Expose Your Ignorance" (page 25) and "Nurture Your Passion" (page 45).

Concrete Skills

Having knowledge is not the same as having the skill and practical ability to apply that knowledge to create software applications. This is where craftsmanship comes in.

—Pete McBreen, Software Craftsmanship

Context

You are seeking a role on a talented team of craftsmen that will provide you with better learning opportunities than you currently have.

Problem

Unfortunately, that team has no incentive to risk hiring someone who may not be able to directly contribute to the team's workload. The team also faces the possibility that you may not even be able to indirectly contribute, such as by automating some simple manual tasks.

Solution

Acquire and maintain concrete skills. Even though one of the things that an apprentice brings to a team is an ability to learn quickly, the possession of discrete and demonstrable ability with specific tools and technologies increases the likelihood that you will be trusted to contribute indirectly until you start to gain stature.

Some of the concrete skills you should acquire will be little more than mechanisms to get you past crude HR filters and managers who construct teams by playing buzzword bingo. Others will reassure your prospective team members that you can be put to good use and will not require "day care" (*Organizational Patterns of Agile Software Development*, p. 88). Examples of concrete skills include writing build files in various popular languages, knowledge of various popular open source frameworks like Hibernate and Struts, basic web design, JavaScript, and the standard libraries in your language of choice.

The point is that you will often require hiring managers to take a leap of faith in choosing you. Concrete skills (which are ideally discrete enough that you can bring toy implementations to an interview) allow you to meet them halfway. The concrete skills you possess are your answer to the question: "If we hire you today, what can you do on Monday morning that will benefit us?" A deep understanding of Your First Language will help establish your credibility and should prove to be extremely useful to your team.

As you begin to make the transition to the role of journeyman you will become less dependent on these skills, as you start to be hired on the basis of your reputation, your portfolio of previous work, and the deeper qualities you bring to a team. Until then, your virtues must be a little more overt.

Dave fills in the gaps

Like most people who come to programming "later" in life, I brought a bunch of life experience with me, far more than your average programmer with six months of experience. I had developed all sorts of interpersonal skills and psychological insights in my previous career. As I progressed as a programmer, I would meet people who would get very excited about my past, and this led me to occasionally overvalue these softer skills, or overpursue nontechnical topics. To be sure, my soft skills have served me well and have helped me tremendously in many situations; however, I have had to let these skills atrophy a bit in order to focus the majority of my attention on developing my technical skills, which was obviously the area where I was most lacking. I didn't switch careers so I could be a therapist to programmers; I switched careers because I love the act of crafting software.

—Dave Hoover

Action

Collect the CVs of people whose skills you respect. You can either ask them for a copy or download the CVs from their websites. For each person, identify five discrete skills noted on the CV, and determine which of these skills would be immediately useful on the kind of team you want to join. Put together a plan and a toy project that will demonstrate that you have acquired these skills. Implement the plan.

Get in the habit of going through your own CV on a regular basis. As you do so, extract the concrete skills into a separate list. Are you comfortable knowing that many hiring managers will only look at the items in this list rather than the sum of your experiences?

See Also

"Your First Language" (page 13).

Expose Your Ignorance

> Tomorrow I need to look stupider and feel better about it.
> This staying quiet and trying to guess what's going on isn't
> working so well.
>
> —Jake Scruggs in "My Apprenticeship at Object Mentor" ‖

‖ *http://www.jikity.com/Blah/apprentice.htm*

Context

The people who are paying you to be a software developer are depending on you to know what you're doing.

Problem

Your managers and team members need confidence that you can deliver, but you are unfamiliar with some of the required technologies. This doesn't just happen to consultants. It happens to everyone. Perhaps you've been brought in because you have a deep understanding of the business domain or some other aspect of the technology stack being used in a team. Or perhaps you're simply the only person available to do the job.

Solution

Show the people who are depending on you that the learning process is part of delivering software. Let them see you grow.

According to research by the social psychologist Carol Dweck, the need to appear competent is ingrained into people of most industrialized societies. These societies are increasingly dependent on your competence as a developer, as software creeps ever-deeper into our everyday lives. Yet because of your inexperience, you have many zones of ignorance. You are in a bind. The people around you—your manager, your client, your colleagues, not to mention yourself—are all under tremendous pressure to deliver software. You can see the need for confidence in people's eyes when they ask you how long feature X will take you to finish. There can be tremendous pressure to pacify them, to reassure them that you know precisely what they want, how you're going to give it to them, and when.

Software craftsmen build their reputations through strong relationships with their clients and colleagues. Conceding to unspoken pressures and telling people what they want to hear is not a good way to build strong relationships. Tell people the truth. Let them know that you're starting to understand what they want and you're in the process of learning how to give it to them. If you reassure them, reassure them with your ability to learn, not by pretending to know something you don't. In this way, your reputation will be built upon your learning ability rather than what you already know.

The most obvious way to expose your ignorance is to ask questions. This is easier said than done, particularly when the person you're asking has assumed that you already know the answer. Press on! Sure, you could protect your pride and take less direct routes to obtain the required knowledge, but remember that your road to journeyman will be shortened by taking the most direct route available. With practice and time, you will find that asking direct questions to the most knowledgeable people on your team will become second nature. While you are exposing your ignorance, you are also exposing your team to your learning ability.

And sometimes they will gain a new clarity about their own knowledge in the process of answering your question.

A "not knowing" stance

As a family therapist I was taught to throw off the notion that I had expert knowledge about other people's lives, to approach people with a "not knowing" stance. This is a hard pill to swallow whether you're a newbie therapist or a newbie programmer. Your instincts tell you to hide your ignorance, to feign expert knowledge, but this only stunts your growth and inhibits the work you are trying to accomplish. Taking this lesson with me from one career to another has served me well. I actually had grown attached to feeling ignorant on a daily basis; it let me know I was in the right place. I was growing.

—Dave Hoover

Get used to this learning process. This is craftsmanship. There are those who are uncomfortable with this process. Rather than becoming craftsmen, these people become experts, people who achieve expertise on one platform or in one domain and stick with it. Because of their narrow focus, experts can deliver functionality into a specific context better than anyone else. It is certainly important and inevitable for our industry to have experts, but that is not the goal of the apprentice.

Expertise is a by-product of the long road we're all on, but it is not the destination. Over the course of their journey, craftsmen will work with countless technologies and domains. If, through necessity or interest, they Dig Deeper and develop expertise in one or more of these technologies, so much the better. This is to be expected, just as the runner training for a marathon develops stronger leg muscles. She's not training to have strong legs; she's training to run. Like the motivated developer who after working on a Python project for two years achieves a deep knowledge of Python, the marathon runner's strong leg muscles are a means, not an end.

Some experts will do everything they can to remain wedded to a single context, narrowing the scope of their learning, their practice, and their projects. Craftsmen, on the other hand, need to have the courage and humility to set aside their expertise and wear The White Belt as they pick up an unfamiliar technology or learn a new domain.

One of the most important traits that a craftsman can possess is the ability to learn, identifying an area of ignorance and working to reduce it. Like bare patches in a garden, ignorance can be reduced by cultivating your seeds of knowledge. Water your seeds through experimentation, practice, and reading. You can choose to hide these bare patches from the light, embarrassed by their size, covering them to keep your pride intact. Or you can choose to expose them, being honest with yourself and the people who are depending on you, and asking for help.

By the end of your apprenticeship, you will have in-depth knowledge of a few threads of technology. With these threads you can weave together robust software applications on a small number of platforms and domains. The master craftsman has the ability to weave a tapestry out of myriad threads. No doubt he will have his favorite threads and his favorite combinations, but the number of threads will be large, allowing the master craftsman to adapt into a wide range of technological environments. This is where The Long Road will take you. By exposing and then confronting your ignorance, you will spin the missing threads much more quickly than you will by faking it in order to appear competent.

Action

Write down a list of five things you really don't understand about your work. Put that list where others can see it. Then get in the habit of refreshing this list as your work changes.

See Also

"Confront Your Ignorance" (page 28), "Dig Deeper" (page 105), and "The Long Road" (page 38).

Confront Your Ignorance

If we value independence, if we are disturbed by the growing conformity of knowledge, of values, of attitudes, which our present system induces, then we may wish to set up conditions of learning which make for uniqueness, for self-direction, and for self-initiated learning.

—Carl Rogers, On Becoming a Person

Context

You have identified gaps in your skillset, gaps that are relevant to your daily work.

Problem

There are tools and techniques that you need to master, but you do not know how to begin. Some of these are things that everyone around you already seems to know, and there is an expectation that you already have this knowledge.

Solution

Pick one skill, tool, or technique and actively fill the gaps in your knowledge about it.

Do this in whichever ways are most effective for you. For some people, the best approach involves trying to get an overview by reading all the introductory articles and FAQs they can get hold of. Other people find that jumping straight to the construction of Breakable Toys is the most effective way to understand something. Whichever approach works for you, don't forget to ask around to your Kindred Spirits and mentors to see if anyone already has this skill and is willing to share what they've learned. Sometimes others will be trying to acquire this skill as well, and by working together you can make better progress. At some point you will have gained a satisfactory level of ability in this new area, and then you can decide whether it is more productive to dig deeper or to turn your attention to the other gaps in your skillset. There aren't enough hours in the day to hone all your skills to a high level, so you must learn to make the necessary trade-offs between them.

This pattern is closely tied to Expose Your Ignorance, but implementing it is less of a challenge to your pride because it can be done in private, without anyone else ever finding out the things you did not know. However, as an apprentice with aspirations to mastery, you need to be willing to Expose Your Ignorance as well. Using this pattern in isolation (that is, confronting your ignorance without exposing it) runs the risk of encouraging a culture where failure and learning are unacceptable because everybody does their learning in secret. Remember that learning in public is one of the ways in which an apprentice begins the transition to journeyman. It's a small step from learning where people can see you to teaching.

Even a successful application of this pattern can have negative side effects. The programmers who maintain your code are unlikely to appreciate it if your need to learn how to build complex concurrent systems leads you to write your own messaging system in Scala rather than using an off-the-shelf product. They're going to be even more upset if they can't ask you any questions about it because you're currently at a conference. Finally, your employer is also unlikely to be understanding if your educational needs get in the way of the successful delivery of its project. In short, you need to be sensitive enough not to let your apprenticeship become a problem for the team. One of the distinguishing facets of the craft approach is a willingness to put the wider interests of your community before your own, rather than using the team and the client to further your personal growth.

On the other hand, it is also possible to Expose Your Ignorance without confronting it. People who do this merely shrug apologetically when confronted by their ignorance, as if to say "that's just the way it is." This leads to a lifetime of being humble, ignorant, and overly dependent on other members of the team. Eventually, it leads to teams where each member defends her own little silo of knowledge and shrugs when a problem crosses into someone else's territory.

So it's important to strike a delicate balance between this pattern and Expose Your Ignorance. Confronting your ignorance on its own leads to arrogant infovores who never get anything done, while exposing your ignorance without seeing it as a problem to be solved leads to excessive humility and helplessness.

Action

Take the list of items from Expose Your Ignorance and strive to learn each one, crossing them off the list as you do so. This new knowledge you have may reveal gaps you hadn't noticed before; don't forget to add these things to your list.

See Also

"Breakable Toys" (page 79), "Expose Your Ignorance" (page 25), and "Kindred Spirits" (page 64).

The Deep End

If you've never fallen on your face, odds are you haven't attempted anything worth a damn.

—Christopher Hawkins, "So You Want To Be a Software Consultant?"#

Context

Taking small, safe steps has left you unsatisfied. You're beginning to fear that this isn't a plateau but a rut. On a plateau, you consolidate your skills through diligent practice in order to attain the next level; in a rut, bland competence eventually decays into mediocrity.

Problem

You need to grow your skills, your confidence, and your portfolio of successful work. You feel the need to challenge yourself with bigger things. This may involve bigger projects, larger teams, more complex tasks, new and business domains, or new places.

Solution

Jump in at the deep end. Waiting until you're ready can become a recipe for never doing a thing. So when you're offered a high-profile role or a difficult problem, grasp it with both hands. Growth only happens by taking on the scary jobs and doing things that stretch you.

This has risks. If you get it wrong and end up over your head you could drown. Thankfully there are many places in IT where you can take risks without destroying your career if you fail. Risks are opportunities seen through the half-shut eyes of fear. This doesn't mean lying

 # http://www.christopherhawkins.com/08-30-2006.htm

on your resume to get a job you can't do, nor does it mean tackling challenges without adequate preparation. Instead, it means taking that promotion or foreign assignment when it's offered, even if the very real possibility of failure is staring you in the face. Being prepared to fail and recovering from that failure opens doors that the timid will never see.

Jumping in with both feet

I came into this Spanish company that did this telecoms service delivery platform. I was on the core team. Normal work but nothing really challenging. There had been a change of CTO and I was quite dissatisfied with the whole direction.

I was getting bored and had made up my mind to leave the company when I heard that we needed a consultant in Nigeria. I mentioned in kitchen talk that I would do it.

I met with the CTO and CEO and they asked me if I was willing to make the change. My contract would change and I would no longer be a normal employee.

They wanted me to sell the company's product but I'm not a salesman. Then I read scary reports about how Lagos was the third most dangerous city in the world. I was really scared about it. But I told myself if it's so horribly dangerous I can always fly back the same day.

Two weeks later I flew there. Talking to a colleague who already lived there before leaving helped. Maybe I'm just bold or stupid but those fears just disappeared. Maybe not in the first day or two but in a matter of weeks I was like a fish in water.

This was supposed to be a small contract for three months but I stayed for nearly two years helping the client. I realized that there was no way we could sell our platform over there. They needed something else. The platform would not help them, so I jumped in and fixed their services and built a platform for them that really suited their needs.

Since Nigeria I've been in almost every West African country. Now I'm working in London.

—Enrique Comba Riepenhausen, email

Even though we advocate seeking out the most challenging tasks you are capable of, you still need to remember that if the water level is above your head it means you're drowning. Even in Enrique's example, where he was changing his life in a big way, he was still moving to a country where he knew at least one person and could speak the national language. It's your responsibility to offset the risks of this approach by Finding Mentors and Kindred Spirits who can provide help when you need it.

It's also your responsibility to Create Feedback Loops, so that if the challenging project starts to spin out of control you can catch it and get help immediately. Applying this pattern should feel brave rather than reckless.

Action

What is the biggest successful project you have ever worked on in terms of lines of code and number of developers? What is the biggest codebase you have ever built on your own? Write down the answers to these questions, and then see if you can find other dimensions of project complexity and other ways of measuring your projects. Use these metrics to measure every project you have ever been involved in. Now, when the next project comes along, you can draw a chart of all your projects and plot where the new project falls among the others. After a while, you will be able to use this chart to see where your career is heading, and even start to make choices based on it.

See Also

"Create Feedback Loops" (page 92), "Find Mentors" (page 61), and "Kindred Spirits" (page 64).

Retreat into Competence

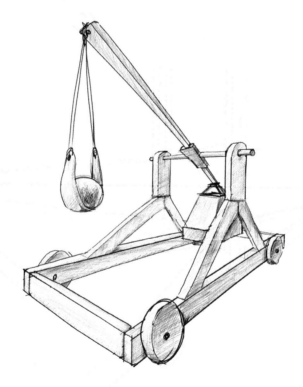

> You look at where you're going and where you are and it
> never makes sense, but then you look back at where
> you've been and a pattern seems to emerge. And if you
> project forward from that pattern, then sometimes you can
> come up with something.
>
> —Robert Pirsig, Zen and the Art of Motorcycle Maintenance

Context

You are beginning to realize how little you know, or perhaps you have taken on a new challenge and things aren't working out so well. Or both.

Problem

As you are introduced to the vast reaches of your ignorance you are overwhelmed.

Solution

Pull back, then launch forward like a stone from a catapult. Retreat briefly into your competence to regain your composure. Take some time to build something that you know how to build. Then use that experience to recognize how far you've come and how much you are currently capable of.

An apprenticeship is a roller-coaster ride. You will experience the thrill of learning new technologies, leveraging your knowledge and creativity to deliver value to your customers. But you will also experience the heart-in-your-throat terror of perceiving just how little you know compared to the craftsmen and experts you meet along the way. It can be overwhelming, particularly when a deadline is looming or when you're dealing with production issues. Take heart. This is a normal and inevitable phenomenon along The Long Road. Overcoming the fear of your own incompetence is the bridge between Expose Your Ignorance and Confront Your Ignorance.

This pattern is most relevant for people who have stretched themselves far beyond their ability. If your apprenticeship has you taking reasonable-sized steps forward, taking on gradually increasing responsibilities and technical complexity, then you may not need to take shelter in this pattern. But if you are really struggling or are barely keeping your head above water in The Deep End, look for opportunities to temporarily retreat. Sometimes you need to take one step back in order to take two steps forward. When you do this, it is important to turn that backward movement into forward momentum as quickly as possible. That forward momentum is revealed in your possession of more knowledge and greater skill than you had yesterday.

Going backward makes this a risky pattern use, however. Without a consciously chosen limit on how long and how far you retreat, you may find yourself merely surrendering to your fear of failure. It can be very comforting to delve ever deeper into the things you know how to do well. The rewards of expertise are tangible and immediate, but the risks may not surface until it's too late to do anything about them. When your expertise eventually becomes obsolete, you will be forced to once again face the vast reaches of your ignorance, but this time you may be out of the habit of learning new things and starting again will be that much more painful. In this scenario, the solution to the feeling of being overwhelmed becomes worse than the problem.

To prevent this from happening, you must accept that this pattern is only a short-term fix while you gather your strength to bounce back. Set a time limit (or "timebox") for yourself, such as "I will spend the next 10 minutes refactoring the JavaScript validation for this page before I optimize the SQL queries that provide the data." Or "I will spend the next four hours implementing the command-line interface for this tool before I learn how to call this third-party SOAP API." Or "I will spend the rest of today improving our test coverage before taking on the job of optimizing our code that is affected by Python's Global Interpreter Lock."

Another important aspect of this solution is to use the temporary break to seek support from the mentors and Kindred Spirits you have gathered around you. With their support and the boost of a recent display of competence, you should be better equipped to handle the inevitable bumps on the road when you try again.

Action

Pick something self-contained that you know really well and reimplement it. For instance, Ade likes to implement caching algorithms because they can range from the trivial to the highly complex. They also allow opportunities to reinforce his intuition about design and algorithmic complexity.

See Also

"Confront Your Ignorance" (page 28), "Expose Your Ignorance" (page 25), "Kindred Spirits" (page 64), and "The Long Road" (page 38).

Wrapping Up

All this talk of ignorance, deep ends, exposure, and retreat might sound negative. But ignorance is not a bad thing if it is recognized and confronted. The worst case is that you're not even aware of your ignorance, but if you recognize what you're missing and address it, you've taken a step forward. One of the foundations of a solid apprenticeship is an Accurate Self-Assessment, in which you try to determine how far along the path you are and take note of any gaps in your knowledge. You need to become intimately familiar with your competencies, the skills you need to immediately become competent in, and the knowledge that interests you long-term. Upcoming patterns such as Reflect as You Work and Record What You Learn should help you maintain this familiarity. Above all, embrace this season of The

Long Road. There are few other times in your career when you can be this inward-focused and dedicated to your own personal growth.

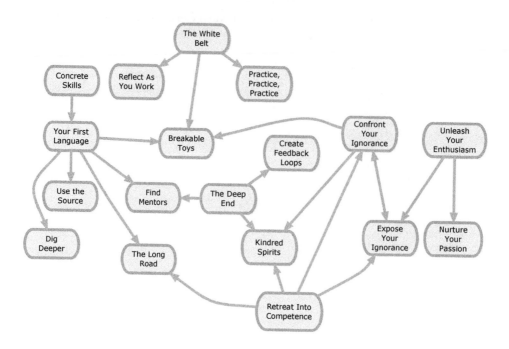

CHAPTER THREE

Walking the Long Road

It's not just a question of conquering a summit previously unknown, but of tracing, step by step, a new pathway to it.

—Gustav Mahler, musician and composer

Do you have training and achievement certificates hanging around your cubicle? Back when Dave had his very own cube and even less experience than he does now, he conspicuously piled a stack of certificates near his desk. The pile featured a Brainbench "master" certification in Perl and grew to include certificates proving that he had completed various multiday trainings in C, J2EE, Vignette, and ATG Dynamo. This small stack of pseudoparchment reassured him (and his organization) that he knew what he was doing. He had been "trained."

Meanwhile, Dave had started to branch out and connect with the broader developer community through *http://perlmonks.org* and the comp.lang.perl.* newsgroups. It was in these groups that he discovered some exceptional Perl hackers. The hackers' expertise was daunting, particularly because Dave could see that they were still learning, and fast. It began to dawn on him that he had barely scratched the surface of what it meant to be a great software developer. Over the following months, his pile of training certificates slowly disappeared beneath a larger pile of scratch paper and printouts of book drafts and tutorials.

Through his observations and interactions with a few of these exceptional hackers, Dave was captured by the learning process. Periodically he would catch a glimpse of the depth and breadth of the hackers' knowledge and come away either discouraged or inspired—discouraged by how little he understood, yet inspired by the power of these hackers' abilities. He threw himself into side projects and began to read anything he could get his hands on.

The more Dave learned, the more he recognized how far he had to go. Over the next few years he had the good fortune to collaborate face-to-face with some exceptional software developers. Dave saw that although these exceptional people were miles ahead of him, they were all walking the same road.

The Long Road

> "How long will it take to master aikido?" a prospective student asks. "How long do you expect to live?" is the only respectable response.
>
> —*George Leonard, Mastery*

> To become truly good at programming is a life's work, an ongoing enterprise of learning and practicing.
>
> —*Ron Jeffries et al., Extreme Programming Installed*

> For every step you take toward mastery, your destination moves two steps further away. Embrace mastery as a lifelong endeavor. Learn to love the journey.
>
> —*George Leonard, Mastery*

Context

We live in a culture that values overnight celebrity, rising stars, material wealth, and quick results. There are very few programmers around who can tell you what software development used to be like back in the old days. When you do speak to these veterans, they shake their heads at the latest industry fad that is repeating the mistakes they saw in their youth. The lessons appear to have been forgotten because there is so little knowledge transferred between generations of software developers.

Problem

You aspire to become a master software craftsman, yet your aspiration conflicts with what people expect from you. Conventional wisdom tells you to take the highest-paying job and the first promotion you can get your hands on, to stop programming and get onto more important work rather than slowly building up your skills.

Solution

First, accept the fact that you may be considered a bit strange for what you want to become. Second, keep your focus on the long term. During your apprenticeship, value learning and long-term growth opportunities over salary and traditional notions of leadership.

People aspiring to become masters of software craftsmanship need to plan for the long term. This long (yet bright) journey will bring you a rich set of abilities. You will become skilled at learning, problem solving, and developing strong relationships with your customers. You will come to wield knowledge and technology as the samurai uses his short and long swords. You will come to comprehend and appreciate the deeper truths of software development. But all this will take time.

You should be prepared for the length of this journey. When you Draw Your Own Map, you should keep in mind the expectation that you will be a working software developer even when you are middle-aged. Let this influence the jobs you take and the scope of your ambitions. If you're still going to be working in 20 years' time, then you can do anything. No one is so far ahead that you can't match their skill level given the decades you will have to hone your craft. No business or technical domain is closed to you. With an entire career devoted to the craft, it becomes realistic rather than vain to think about surpassing people like Donald Knuth or Linus Torvalds. The length of the journey merely multiplies the possibilities that are open to you. (Of course, people like Knuth and Torvalds won't be staying still whilst you catch up to them!)

This pattern is not for people aspiring to become CIOs or project managers, or filthy rich. Along the way, it is not unlikely that you will take on roles of power and responsibility or find yourself quite wealthy. However, these roles and benefits are not the main motivation of the successful apprentice—they are merely by-products of a lifelong journey. And rather than counting the days to retirement, the craftsman will willingly and joyfully work into her final decades.

We don't want to give the impression that everyone must follow a single road (see Draw Your Own Map) or that this is the right road for every software developer (see A Different Road). Some people leave development permanently and become executives, testers, salespeople, or project managers. Some people leave technology permanently and enter into entirely different fields. These are all valid and beneficial roads to take, but this book and this pattern are not for those people.

If an Accurate Self-Assessment is the cornerstone of a successful apprenticeship, then The Long Road is the foundation. The transition from apprentice to journeyman is only the first of many steps along the path to mastery. Like a martial artist attaining the rank of black belt, a new journeyman realizes how much farther he has to go.

Software developers are fortunate. Ours is a complex and profound path, a path that by its nature changes continually. Moore's Law marches relentlessly on, regularly opening up new opportunities for craftsmen to explore new platforms or reprioritize the characteristics of an established program. And yet, other changes are often superficial. New technologies replace older technologies, yet solve the same fundamental problems. While there will always be new software to learn and better hardware just around the corner, The Long Road teaches craftsmen the deeper truths of the craft, allowing the masters to transcend specific technologies and cut to the heart of the problem.

Action

Close your eyes and imagine the strangest possible role you could be playing in 10 years' time. Have fun thinking of the wackiest possible future for yourself. Then think about 20, 30, and 40 years from now. What kinds of experiences do you want to have tried? Imagine that 40 years from now you are asked to write a short description of your professional history and the biggest influences on your path. Use the output from that thought experiment to help you plan your future career choices.

See Also

"A Different Road" (page 53) and "Draw Your Own Map" (page 47).

Craft over Art

> **I would describe programming as a craft, which is a kind of art, but not a fine art. Craft means making useful objects with perhaps decorative touches. Fine art means making things purely for their beauty.**
>
> —*Richard Stallman in "Art and Programming"* *

Context

You are being paid to build something that will solve a problem for a customer.

Problem

Although there is a proven solution available, your customer's problem represents an opportunity to do something truly fantastic, providing you with an opportunity to create something beautiful that will impress your colleagues.

Solution

Craftsmanship is built upon strong relationships. Focus on delivering value to your customer over advancing your own self-interests.

As a craftsman you are primarily building something that serves the needs of others, not indulging in artistic expression. After all, there's no such thing as a starving craftsman. As our friend Laurent Bossavit put it: "For a craftsman to starve is a failure; he's supposed to earn a living at his craft."[†] You need to do your best work in ways that place the interests of your customers over your desire to display skill or pad your resume, while still adhering to the minimum standards of competence provided by the software development community. Walking the Long Road means you must balance these conflicting demands. If you starve because you are too much of an artist and your creations are too beautiful to be delivered in the real world, then you have left the craft. If your desire to do beautiful work forces you out of professional software development and away from building useful things for real people, then you have left the craft.

The things we build for customers *can* be beautiful, but *must* be useful. Part of the process of maturation encompassed by this pattern is developing the ability to sacrifice beauty in favor of utility if and when it becomes necessary.

Indulging in the creation of beautiful but useless artifacts is not craftsmanship. A craftsman values a fifty-line game that makes someone smile over a million-line game that pushes the frontiers of computer science but is unplayable.

Another aspect of craft over art is that your customers need you to produce satisfactory quality even when you don't feel like it. A craftsman is unwilling to wait until inspiration strikes before she delivers artifacts that satisfy her customers. This has both positive and negative connotations. On the one hand, the craftsman is barred from the idyllic playground of art, where other people pay her to build the things she wants. On the other hand, she and her customers have the satisfaction of creating and using software that provides immediate value.

* John Littler, "Art and Computer Programming." Available at: *http://www.onlamp .com/pub/a/onlamp/2005/06/30/artofprog.html*.

† Laurent Bossavit, personal communication.

Ken on craftsmanship

Working on real problems for real people is what hones the craft, not just doing it for self-satisfaction.

—Ken Auer, email

This pattern is not about doing merely what is expedient. It also encompasses the idea that a useful craft artifact always displays at least a minimal level of quality. When using this pattern you will have to balance your customer's desire for the immediate resolution of their problem with the internal standards that make you a craftsman. Being able to hold on to these standards even when you are under pressure requires you to develop an understanding that utility and beauty are not opposed, but interdependent. The more useful a piece of software, the more important it is that the software be high quality. But quality takes time. You will have to work toward a suitable level of quality by repeatedly making trade-offs between beauty and utility. Sometimes you will make the wrong trade-off, and fixing that mistake by rewriting the system from scratch may not be in the customer's best interest. In those situations you will need to develop the ability to refactor and repair. As Sennet wrote, "it is by fixing things that we often get to understand how they work."‡ In this case, the time spent on fixes when you have veered too far toward either art or expediency will teach you lessons about software development that cannot be learned in any other way.

Action

In the next 24 hours, find an opportunity to do something useful rather than beautiful. This may be a straightforward choice, or it may involve a more subtle trade-off. The important thing is to make yourself aware of the issues discussed here when you choose what to do.

Another way to improve your awareness is to think of situations over the last year where you chose artistry over utility. How did that turn out? Write down what you think would have happened if you had made a different choice.

See Also

"The Long Road" (page 38).

‡ *The Craftsman*, p. 199

Sustainable Motivations

Anyone who has ever seen a programmer at work...knows that programming itself, if the programmer is given the chance to do it his way, is the biggest motivation in programming.

—*Jerry Weinberg, The Psychology of Computer Programming*

Context

As an apprentice, you must develop your technical skills. Because of this you will often find yourself working in the messy realities of ambiguously specified projects for customers with shifting and conflicting demands.

Problem

Working in the trenches of real-world projects is rigorous, sometimes tedious, sometimes exhausting, often frustrating, and frequently overly chaotic or constraining.

Solution

Ensure that your motivations for craftsmanship will adapt and survive through the trials and tribulations of The Long Road.

There will be days, weeks, and months when you love your job. You'll chuckle to yourself, in awe that you actually get *paid* to develop software. The software you write will flow effortlessly from your mind through your fingertips, beautiful to behold in function and design. These are good and extraordinary days. In other words, they are not your ordinary days.

> ...there is not much overlap between the kind of software that makes money and the kind of software that's interesting to write.... If you want to make money, you tend to be forced to work on problems that are too nasty for anyone to solve for free.
>
> —Paul Graham, *Hackers & Painters*

As Paul Graham so rightly says, the typical programming job will put you face-to-face with tedious, vaguely defined, and needlessly complex problems. Nasty, wicked problems. What's more, you may also be faced with bureaucracy, difficult personalities, and spotty leadership. There will be days, weeks, and months when you question your commitment to the craft. When you are confronted with such problems, it is crucial that your motivations to program are aligned with walking The Long Road. Here are a few examples to illustrate the point:

- You hate your programming job and you're motivated primarily by money. You find yourself focusing on climbing the corporate ladder over honing your craftsmanship. But you are also motivated by your reputation as a technologist, and this allows you to endure long enough for your job situation to improve.

- You're motivated primarily by your enjoyment of programming, but you've had a few months when you can't feel the love. You are seriously considering abandoning the profession. Fortunately, you are also motivated by money, and you think that programming is your best option financially right now. You stick it out for the money and eventually your love for programming returns.

- Your work on open source projects is motivated primarily by a desire to build your reputation. While your projects provide value to users around the world, your status as a hacker has remained stagnant and you are considering abandoning your work. Yet, your belief in the importance of free software keeps you going. Your projects eventually blossom and your reputation grows.

Some programmers become inadvertently trapped by their motivations. In *More Secrets of Consulting*, Dorset House, Jerry Weinberg describes this phenomenon as the Golden Lock: "I'd like to learn something new, but what I already know pays too well." The risk of the Golden Lock highlights the importance of aligning your motivations with The Long Road, which requires the ambition to achieve mastery. A desire for mastery should motivate you to be wary of Golden Locks as they inevitably present themselves. As you progress as a craftsman, you will be faced with tough decisions that will determine whether you have the freedom to stay on The Long Road or whether you will find yourself trapped in a Golden Lock. Two examples:

Obie Fernandez is an exceptional Java programmer whose reputation was built on his Java expertise. Obie had a decision to make in 2005: continue to grow his Java-expert status, or learn a promising new web framework (Rails) in an unfamiliar language (Ruby). Obie chose to focus on learning in order to expand his toolset. This is the mark of a craftsman. He set aside the safety of his Java reputation and became a Ruby newbie, avoiding a Golden Lock. Ironically, this decision allowed Obie to ascend to even greater heights than his previous Java-expert status, and eventually led him to start the web application development firm Hashrocket.

On a couple of occasions, Marten Gustafson has found himself in the midst of a project death march because his passion for the craft induced him to throw all of his time and energy into the project. Marten is not the first nor the last young programmer to throw himself into this bottomless pit with the good intention of heroically saving the day. If you are walking The Long Road to mastery, it is essential that you Nurture Your Passion for software craftsmanship while keeping it in balance with the other aspects of your life. Naturally, there will be times where the scales will tip in one direction or another. Nevertheless, you should be conscious of this balancing act all along The Long Road.

Dave's low pain threshold

During the evolution of this pattern, David Wood (one of my Kindred Spirits from my ThoughtWorks days) shared some conventional wisdom with me: "Do what you love and the money will follow." This advice resonates with me because I am a complete wuss when I can't do what I love. On the flip side, when I'm doing what I love, I find that I have an overwhelming amount of creativity and energy to throw into my work, which ultimately provides me with greater financial rewards. While many programmers could probably find higher-paying jobs in the short term, the money that follows from doing what you love will pay off handsomely in the long run. To read more about this unconventional wisdom, check out the commencement address to Stanford's class of 2005 by none other than (college dropout and Apple cofounder) Steve Jobs.§

—Dave Hoover

Action

Write down at least 15 things that motivate you. Wait a little while, then write down another five. How many of your motivations are about what other people think rather than what you feel? Are the percentages different between your first 15 and the final 5? How many of the motivating factors can you do without? Now write down a list of the five most important things that motivate you. Keep that list somewhere that you can look at it when times get tough.

See Also

"Nurture Your Passion" (page 45) and "The Long Road" (page 38).

Nurture Your Passion

> **To only a fraction of the human race does God give the privilege of earning one's bread doing what one would have gladly pursued free, for passion. I am very thankful.**
>
> —Frederick Brooks, *The Mythical Man-Month*

Context

You have been hired as "just" a software developer.

Problem

You work in an environment that stifles your passion for the craft.

§ *http://news-service.stanford.edu/news/2005/june15/jobs-061505.html*

Solution

Take steps to protect and grow your passion for software craftsmanship.

To become a journeyman, you will need to have a passion for software craftsmanship. Unfortunately, your daily activities often work to diminish this passion. You might be faced with demoralizing corporate hierarchies, project death marches, abusive managers, or cynical colleagues. It's hard for your passion to grow when exposed to such hostile conditions, but there are some basic actions you can take to sustain it.

Work on what you like. Find something at work that interests you, identify it as something you enjoy, and pour yourself into it. If you can't spare enough time during the workday for this activity, consider putting in some extra time. If this isn't feasible, dedicate some time outside of work to build some Breakable Toys.

In a presentation at O'Reilly's Open Source Convention (OSCON) 2004 entitled *Great Hackers*, Paul Graham said, "The key to being a great hacker may be to work on what you like.... To do something well you have to love it. So to the extent that you can preserve hacking as something you love, you're likely to do it well."

Seek out Kindred Spirits. Join a local user group that focuses on something you want to learn more about. Start a weblog and read blogs that interest you. Participate in online forums and mailing lists and Share What You Learn. Start a study group using the Knowledge Hydrant pattern language from Joshua Kerievsky's paper "A Pattern Language for Study Groups."‖

Study the Classics. Immersing yourself in some of the great literature of our field can carry you through the rough spots when your passion is in jeopardy. These timeless books can open your eyes to a different world, a world where things can be better.

Draw Your Own Map. There are times when your needs, goals, and aspirations contradict the career paths your employer provides. Moving into an organization that offers career paths congruent with your own can protect your passion.

Project death marches are probably the most damaging of the hostile conditions. It's hard to imagine how you could protect your passion, let alone grow it, in the face of a death march. It saps your time and your energy, preventing you from taking any significant actions to protect your passion as more important issues like personal health and strained relations at home demand your attention. Death marches play into the hero mentality that is prevalent in many software development organizations. The people who walk The Long Road are not the heroes who sprint for a few years and burn out—they are the people moving at a sustainable pace for decades.

To grow your passion, set clear boundaries that define the sort of environment you are willing to work in. This might mean you leave work while the rest of the team stays late, that you walk out of a meeting that has become abusive, that you steer a cynical conversation toward

‖ *http://www.industriallogic.com/papers/khdraft.pdf*

constructive topics, or that you refuse to distribute code that doesn't meet your minimum standards. The result could be that you get passed over for pay raises, promotions, kudos, or popularity. But these boundaries are necessary if you are going to break free of hostile conditions and keep your passion strong.

Later in his OSCON presentation, Paul Graham went on to say, "Try to keep the sense of wonder about programming that you had at age 14. If you're worried that your current job is rotting your brain, it probably is."

> The traveler whose main path of mastery coincides with career and livelihood is fortunate; others must find space and time outside regular working hours for a preferred practice that brings mastery but not a living wage.
>
> —George Leonard, *Mastery*, p. 133

Action

On your way to work prepare a list of three positive ideas to talk about. During the day, if the conversation starts to sap your energy, steer it to one of these three topics. The aim is to take control and avoid being dragged down by the negative conversations around you. On the way home, review your level of success and think about other ways to improve your environment.

See Also

"Draw Your Own Map" (page 47), "Kindred Spirits" (page 64), "Study the Classics" (page 104), and "The Long Road" (page 38).

Draw Your Own Map

> **Beware of the detractors. We might come across situations or colleagues or people in the society who will try to prove that programming...will become an unsustainable activity as time passes by. They think software development is only for fresh graduates...and when we get married and have kids we cannot do that anymore.**
>
> —*Mohan Radhakrishnan, comment #*

http://apprenticeship.oreilly.com/wiki/show/draw_your_own_map (must register and log in)

Context

Any given employer can offer only a limited subset of all possible career paths.

Problem

None of the career paths that your employer provides fits for you.

Solution

Identify a logical but ambitious next step for your career. Understand that it's not up to your employer, your career counselor, or your professors to give you a hand up. Arriving at your next step and charting the course to ultimately arrive at your ideal destination is your responsibility. With your next career step identified, visualize the smaller, interim steps you need to take to move forward.

It is vitally important that you take the first step even if it doesn't seem that significant. That first step will generate the momentum that will help carry you toward your goals. It's the willingness to take that first terrifying step (and all the other steps later on), even in the absence of a perfect plan, that turns your map from a daydream into reality.

Rather than simply writing down high-level goals, try to define small, achievable steps. These small steps will provide feedback that you can use to modify your map, but they also make it easier to get help from Kindred Spirits to achieve your goals. After all, there's not much anybody else can do to help you become what Paul Graham calls "a great hacker," but they can point you toward resources that will help you learn Lisp or Unix socket programming or achieve similarly well-defined goals.

If you find that your vision of yourself is not in accord with your employer's vision for you, and there doesn't seem to be a way to reconcile the differences, examine other opportunities to see if they're heading in the desired direction. Remember, there isn't one single path that all apprentices follow. Instead, successful apprentices follow paths that share a certain family resemblance. These resemblances do not happen because apprentices are inexorably shepherded into making the same decisions by their mentors. They happen because each apprentice, consciously or not, chooses their route through life based on an overlapping set of values.

You should continuously reassess your map as your circumstances and values change. Sometimes your map will be in accord with that of those around you, and sometimes your map will require you to chart your own path through the wilderness. Some apprentices we've spoken to have found that being open about their current map has enabled them to find Kindred Spirits while maintaining healthy relationships with current and past employers. The only constant is that the map is always yours, and you're free to redraw it at any time.

Use Sustainable Motivations and Use Your Title to prevent your current title and salary from narrowing the possible destinations on your map. If you need to move into a less hierarchically impressive role in order to stay "on the map," consider The Long Road and compare the relative importance of impressive (short-term) titles and salaries to working in a company that is more congruent with your goals and will lead you greater heights in the long term.

Desi draws her own map

I took a job working at a startup company doing all sorts of things including database management, system administration, quality assurance, source control, and even some project management. The role changed over the years and after a while I started to feel the itch to try my hand at programming again. I started out with SQL scripts, Perl scripts, and some shell scripting. These scripts revolved around all of the other duties I mentioned above. I realized that programming was actually fun when you had the time to spend in learning what you were doing and didn't have the pressures of an actual class. I was happy with this for a while but the pressure from my boss on me to become more systems-oriented started to conflict with my desire to move into development. I lost motivation for programming because my job demanded other types of learning and work. I was frustrated because it was not the work I wanted to be doing but I felt that I had managed to get myself stuck. I wanted to leave production operations and system administration behind or at least only do it as a side effect of writing code but the company I was working for would not allow me to make that move. I was having a difficult time finding a job as a developer due to the fact that I had been out of school for 4 years but had no real programming experience. I left the company and went to another company and continued in a configuration management role. I started to try to introduce Perl to this new company and I was met with a very large resistance. I realized that I would have to make another move because my desire to write code was getting stronger. Fortunately ThoughtWorks decided to take a chance on me.

—Desi McAdam, email

Chris pushes the learning limit

At Intrado, Dave Oberto taught me everything I know about SQL. He was the migration lead, and I was the test lead, and he was an amazing programmer. Frank DeSuza taught me everything I know about C, pointer arithmetic, and all the stuff close to the machine. We often employed a contractor named Doug who taught me all I know about software design. I learned a huge amount working there. This annoyed the people around me. I finally left when I was told flat-out that I would not be allowed to learn any more, and that, while I'd been highly successful by exceeding my job description and breaking the boundaries between testers and developers, there were limits—I wouldn't be able to learn to code there. So I left.

—Chris McMahon, email

These stories point to Desi and Chris's priorities. They weren't going to allow a company's expectations or culture to stand in the way of achieving their goal of becoming a better programmer. These stories are particularly appropriate for system administrators and testing professionals who aspire to become developers. Too many organizations pigeonhole people and take a short-sighted approach to their personnel (or "resources"). Thinking of Desi as simply "a sysadmin" is easier to manage than realizing that Desi is a person who aspires to become a great programmer. Some organizations will be able to rally behind the audacious goals their people set for themselves. Other organizations choose not to. If this is the case at your organization, you need to begin to look elsewhere by Expanding Your Bandwidth and Finding Mentors who can provide guidance.

Action

List three jobs that you think you could do following your current one. Then list three jobs each of those could lead to. Take a hard look at all 12 jobs. Is this really the full range of desirable jobs for the next few years of your life? Is there something missing? Extend this diagram by adding three jobs for each of the nine jobs you recently added. This should increase the number of jobs in your diagram by 27. Ask yourself if this set of jobs is more representative of the range of career options you have and the places you want to take your career. What are the constraints that are limiting your options?

If you're unhappy with the diagram so far, repeat the exercise with different jobs, perhaps in different business or technology domains. Then try the exercise yet again and see what happens if you relax one of the constraints that you've always accepted. What if you become willing to move to another country, get a new qualification, or learn a new human/programming language? What if you were to start your own business? What if that business merely used software as a means to an end? There are more possibilities than you might think.

See Also

"Expand Your Bandwidth" (page 74), "Find Mentors" (page 61), "Kindred Spirits" (page 64), "Sustainable Motivations" (page 43), "The Long Road" (page 38), and "Use Your Title" (page 50).

Use Your Title

> **I'm promoting you from Senior Engineer to Lead Engineer.**
>
> **The pay is the same but people will disrespect you less.**
>
> —Dilbert's Pointy-Haired Boss

Context

As a result of your dedication to learning, you have been hired or promoted (formally or informally) into a position with a title containing words such as "senior," "architect," or "lead."

Problem

Your job title doesn't match what you see in the mirror. When you introduce yourself in a professional setting, you feel as if you have to apologize or explain away the difference between your skill level and your job description.

Solution

Do not allow your title to affect you. It is a distraction that should be kept on the outskirts of your consciousness. Use your title to gauge your organization, not yourself.

Don't be fooled by an impressive title. Your mother might think you deserve it, but impressive titles and responsibilities do not indicate that your apprenticeship is over. They only serve to remind you that there is a shortage of craftsmen in our industry.

The other side of the coin is an unimpressive title despite the fact that you have surpassed your colleagues. Like the flattery of an impressive title, the frustration that comes from a lack of recognition should remind you that our industry has a problem. Again, use this situation to measure your organization and its fit for you rather than allowing the frustration to slow you down.

Another variant of this theme is informal versus formal titles. For instance, you may have grown into a position of authority on your team, despite your formal title remaining the same. These informal titles can be hard to ignore, because they are constantly reinforced by your peers, even if they conflict with your self-assessment. During these times, your connections with your mentors and Kindred Spirits will be critical to keep you grounded in reality.

> *Dave sees the sign*
>
> Two years after I wrote my first program, a Perl CGI script, my title was "Senior Application Developer." Having developed a fairly accurate self-assessment, I saw the humor in my situation. Rather than believing that I had achieved my goals, I saw this title as a sign that I needed to move on, to Draw My Own Map.
>
> —Dave Hoover

Action

Write down a long and descriptive version of your job title. Make sure it accurately reflects what you really do at work and your skill level. Keep this updated, and from time to time imagine how you would view a stranger who had this job description.

See Also

"Draw Your Own Map" (page 47) and "Kindred Spirits" (page 64).

Stay in the Trenches

Seduced by the siren song of a consumerist, quick-fix society, we sometimes choose a course of action that brings only the illusion of accomplishment, the shadow of satisfaction.

—*George Leonard, Mastery*

Context

As a result of your dedication to learning, you have established a reputation as someone who can effectively deliver software. Within your organization, exceptional work is rewarded with promotions up the hierarchy.

Problem

You have been offered a promotion into a role that will pull you away from programming.

Solution

The offer of a promotion will test whether you have Sustainable Motivations and are willing to walk The Long Road. Most people equate promotion into management with success. They assume that taking a promotion into management is a no-brainer, a sign that you are on the right path. Aspiring craftsmen must not be fooled into believing that they will remain a "technical manager" for long. As Pete McBreen wrote, "as soon as a person stops practicing, her mastery fades." Every day that you are not programming is another step away from becoming a journeyman.

So to remain on that path, work with your employer to find other mechanisms for rewarding you. These may include more pay or nontraditional technical leadership roles such as internal consultancy. If your organization is inflexible, then it is better to seek opportunities elsewhere (see Draw Your Own Map) than to permit yourself to be promoted away from the craft.

Staying in the trenches is a way to Nurture Your Passion for software development. When you accept a promotion that allows you to continue programming full time, remember to Use Your Title.

It's very easy to apply this pattern in a selfish way by being blind to the needs of those around you. However, as you become a more experienced apprentice you may find yourself trying to change your working environment so that others can keep doing what they love. This can easily become a full-time job unless you're careful to maintain the balance or find ways to create a self-sustaining environment for increasingly senior programmers.

Action

How does your employer reward excellence? If their current rewards aren't appealing, start thinking of other ways they could reward you. Consider whether there are standard constraints that could be loosened in your case. Perhaps there are restrictive clauses in your contract or you have a radical idea that needs sponsorship. Prepare a list of these alternative rewards so that when you reject that promotion, you're in a position to negotiate based on a clear understanding of your own motivations.

See Also

"Draw Your Own Map" (page 47), "Nurture Your Passion" (page 45), "Sustainable Motivations" (page 43), "The Long Road" (page 38), and "Use Your Title" (page 50).

A Different Road

**Just because they're not on your road doesn't mean
they've gotten lost.**

—H. Jackson Brown Jr., Life's Little Instruction Book

Context

You have used Draw Your Own Map and followed it diligently.

Problem

The map you have drawn leads you away from The Long Road.

Solution

Follow your own map and remember what you learned during your apprenticeship.

You have been walking The Long Road for some time. But now as a consequence of Drawing Your Own Map you have realized that this road is no longer a suitable choice for you. You have found another path that has rewards more in tune with your current values: more time with your family or more money, or perhaps a new vocation has captured your attention. Whatever it is, it means saying goodbye to the craft and The Long Road. This may or may not be permanent.

Even if you leave the road permanently, the values and principles you have developed along the way will always be with you. As Dave found out when he ceased to be a family therapist, he couldn't make Prospero's choice (burning his books and breaking his staff), but instead brought the lessons and experiences from that vocation to his new craft. The same applies to you.

When we interviewed Ivan Moore, Ade's mentor since ThoughtWorks, he described how he went off to a Greek island for six months to become a windsurfing instructor after his first IT job. He found that he liked teaching windsurfing, but it wasn't entirely satisfying because he never got to use his brain. Afterward, it was hard for him to get back into the industry because "most HR people in big companies didn't like it."

We have colleagues who have left software development to become teachers, windsurfing instructors, and full-time parents. We respected their choices. If and when they came back, we welcomed them with open arms because those experiences had given them new perspectives they could share. Sadly, conventional software organizations may not be so welcoming. They often see these detours as suspicious gaps in your career that you must justify. They will expect you to have a rationale that makes sense within their value system for why you left and why you're coming back.

Despite this risk, don't be afraid to do something different with your life. If you walk away from software development, you will find that the habit of rigorous thinking and automating tasks involving large volumes of data will still be useful wherever you go. Your past as a software craftsman can enrich whatever future you choose.

Larry's detour through family therapy

In a sense, I can't stay away from the people issues any more than I can stay away from computers. I thought I had escaped when I bid farewell to the computer field in July of 1976, declaring my independence even as America celebrated the bicentennial of its independence. Trained as a family therapist, I ended up spending more than a decade in private practice and agency practice working with couples and families and troubled adolescents. But the forces of the universe conspired to steer me back toward the technological frontier.

—Larry Constantine, *The Peopleware Papers*

Action

If for some reason you could no longer be a software developer, what would you do? Write down some of the other jobs you think you would enjoy doing. Find people who are doing those jobs and loving it. Ask them what they love about it and compare that to the things you love about software development.

See Also

"Draw Your Own Map" (page 47) and "The Long Road" (page 38).

Wrapping Up

The patterns that directly support an apprentice's journey on The Long Road can be assembled into myriad combinations. Their ordering in this chapter does not imply a linear progression. For example...

You may be walking The Long Road with relative ease. Your working environment is not stifling you, your passion for the craft is strong. You are excelling. You receive a promotion to what your organization calls "architect" and you are still programming full time. Your Accurate Self-Assessment suggests that it's time to Use Your Title to gauge the level of your organization. This may be enough to keep you on The Long Road, and perhaps no other patterns are needed.

...or...

Your organization emphasizes financial rewards. There is a constant, unspoken organizational undercurrent that pressures people to focus on making more money; after all, making more money implies you're more valuable to the company. You recognize the undercurrent and the danger it presents to your journey. You Nurture Your Passion and focus on maintaining Sustainable Motivations. Your focus on Craft over Art has grown your reputation, and you are offered a promotion to project manager. By Staying in the Trenches and Drawing Your Own Map, you work with your employer to define a career path that will keep you on The Long Road.

...or...

You have been programming since you were very young. You program because you enjoy creating beautiful, elegant solutions. But now, in the corporate world, you are faced with tasks that are not enjoyable and with customers who need you to deliver functionality and who don't care about elegance. You recognize that for the foreseeable future, your motivation for programming is not aligned with The Long Road. You take steps to Nurture Your Passion as you develop more Sustainable Motivations by focusing on Craft over Art. Over time, you gradually develop a motivation to establish strong relationships with your customers.

As you can see, the possibilities for combining these patterns are as limitless as the contexts that apprentices live within.

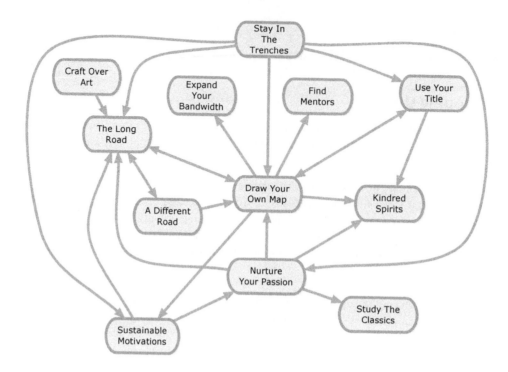

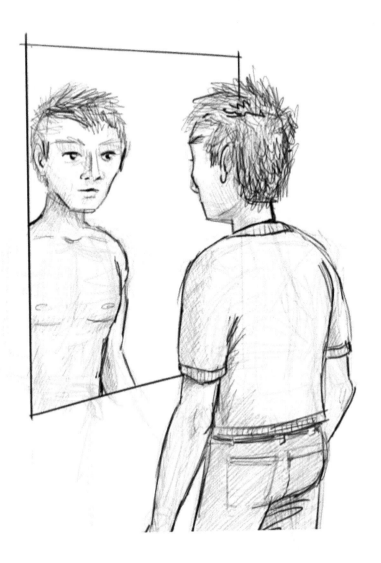

CHAPTER FOUR

Accurate Self-Assessment

One of the primary risks for someone who learns quickly is becoming a big fish in a small pond. While there is nothing inherently wrong with small ponds or big fish, it is critical for the big fish to be aware of other ponds within the vast global network of ponds, and more importantly, the existence of enormous fish, fish that even exceed the size of your little pond.

The talented and hard-working apprentice must not become self-satisfied with his success. It is very easy to rise above the mediocre in the field of software development because too many people become satisfied with staying only slightly ahead of the curve. You must fight this tendency toward mediocrity by seeking out and learning about other teams, organizations, journeymen, and master craftsmen that work at a level of proficiency that an apprentice cannot even imagine.

You must be willing to let go of your perceived competence and allow yourself to recognize that you have traveled only a short distance on The Long Road. Your goal isn't to become better than the "average developer." Your goal is to measure your abilities and find ways to be better than you were yesterday. We're all on the same journey, and comparing ourselves to others is useful only when it allows us to find ways to help each other improve.

Be the Worst

Be the lion's tail rather than the fox's head!

—*Tractate Avot*

Context

You have Unleashed Your Enthusiasm and taken every opportunity to learn new skills. As a result, you have outgrown your team and possibly your entire development organization.

Problem

Your rate of learning has leveled off.

Solution

Surround yourself with developers who are better than you. Find a stronger team where you are the weakest member and have room to grow.

Be the Worst was the seminal pattern of this pattern language. It was lifted from some advice that Pat Metheny offered to young musicians: "Be the worst guy in every band you're in."[*] Pat's advice struck a chord with Dave, and was one of the reasons he started writing this book.

> *Dave finds a better team*
>
> My first programming job was at a dot-com startup. Five months later, the dot-bomb exploded. After the smoke cleared, I landed in the IT department of a large nonprofit organization. It was a great place to weather the downturn for a few years, but compared to my former employer the development pace was excruciatingly slow. Two years later I had learned a ton, but I was unchallenged and had lost hope for significant organizational improvement. Acting as the technical architect of my team initially provided some great learning experiences, but the absurdity of me in an architectural role drove me to look elsewhere for work. The sole purpose of my job search was to increase my rate of learning and the best way I knew to do that was to surround myself with exceptional developers. A year later I was fortunate enough to find myself on a team with several world-class developers. It was an incredible challenge, but a priceless opportunity.
>
> —Dave Hoover

Being in a strong team can make you *feel* as if you are performing better. The other members of that team will often prevent you from making mistakes, and help you recover from mistakes so smoothly that you won't realize that you may not be learning as much as you think. It's only when you work on your own that you will see how much your team increases your productivity and realize how much you have learned. This makes Reflecting as You Work and building Breakable Toys particularly important for people who are the worst on their team. Both provide opportunities to take a step back from the team environment to see what habits, techniques, and knowledge you're picking up from Rubbing Elbows with your more experienced teammates.

The drawing shows that as the weakest member of the team, you should be working harder than anyone else. This is because the goal is not to *stay* the weakest, but to start at the bottom and work your way up. You do this by consciously finding ways to improve and mimicking

---

[*] Chris Morris's blog, "Be The Worst." Available at: *http://clabs.org/blogki/index.cgi?page=/TheArts/BeTheWorst*.

the stronger developers until you are on the same level as the rest of the team. Without this conscious attention to learning from the team, you will face several risks.

First, there is the risk that you will drag the team down. Second, since good teams won't tolerate (for long) someone who is just a passenger, you run the risk of being fired if you're so far behind that you can't catch up or don't seem to be catching up quickly enough. Another side effect of joining a strong team is that you can end up feeling bad about yourself and your skill level unless you're actively honing your skills. At its best, this can motivate you to improve. But like any "sink or swim" strategy, when it fails you will find yourself drowning. This is why it is essential to Create Feedback Loops so that you can tell when you're in trouble. This feedback will tell you if the team is too far ahead of you or hostile to people trying to work their way up.

Like Stay in the Trenches, Be the Worst clashes with cultural norms that encourage you to attain a position of superiority as fast as you can. But as an apprentice, you should value opportunities to learn the craft over expanding and asserting your authority. Sometimes that means you're leading a team (see The Deep End), but as an apprentice, you should typically look to be led.

There is a selfish aspect to purposely joining a team as the worst member. To counter this, complement Be the Worst with Sweep the Floor and Concrete Skills. Sweep The Floor means to explicitly seek out menial tasks in order to directly add value to the project. Developing Concrete Skills will increase your contributions to the development effort and is fundamental to your role as an apprentice. Without these kinds of contributions, this pattern can lead to strong teams being fatally weakened, as Jamie Zawinski points out in his infamous open resignation letter from the Mozilla project.[†] Ultimately, your (rapidly) increasing contribution to the team is why these strong teams will take the risk of bringing you on board.

Jake Scruggs says it well when he speaks of his summer apprenticeship at Object Mentor:

> Without a doubt the coolest thing about working at Object Mentor was being able to lean over and ask David, or Micah, or Paul, or James, or ... Look, everybody sitting next to me had great ideas about programming and, as cool as all their classes are, working with great programmers is a much better way to learn. [‡]

Collaborating with great developers will help you maintain a more accurate self-assessment as well as provide help in Finding Mentors. However, this pattern is usually inappropriate for more experienced developers who are looking to become journeymen. At that stage, you should be looking to mentor novices and give others the opportunities you have been given.

---

† Resignation and postmortem: *http://www.jwz.org/gruntle/nomo.html*.

‡ Jake Scruggs, "My Apprenticeship at Object Mentor." Available at: *http://www.jikity.com/Blah/apprentice.htm*.

Joining Obtiva put me back at the bottom of the food chain. Now, I'm a green Software Apprentice and it'll be awhile before I head a team of developers. Instead of leading I'll be learning. I've been demoted.

Why would someone choose that?

First, being the worst on a team of outstanding developers can't be compensated for with environment, equipment, or money. You can't compensate for learning next to people who have already traveled the path and know how to avoid the holes on the road ahead. Pairing with great software developers is invaluable. If you're new to programming and have not had the opportunity to pair then you need to demand the experience. §

Action

List all the teams you know. Include open source projects, other departments, and other companies. Sort these teams by skill level, then identify a team that is open to new members who want to work their way up. This may require you to join several mailing lists and ask various people questions in order to gauge their relative skill level. At the end of the process you will be better at comparing skill levels, and may even have a new team!

See Also

"Breakable Toys" (page 79), "Concrete Skills" (page 24), "Create Feedback Loops" (page 92), "Find Mentors" (page 61), "Reflect As You Work" (page 85), "Rubbing Elbows" (page 66), "Stay in the Trenches" (page 52), "Sweep the Floor" (page 68), "The Deep End" (page 30), and "Unleash Your Enthusiasm" (page 22).

Find Mentors

Whether a beginner starts out with a training course or is self-taught, the first step on the path to software craftsmanship is finding a craftsman to apprentice himself to.

—Pete McBreen, Software Craftsmanship, p. 96

§ Brian Tatnall, "New beginnings with Obtiva." Available at: *http://syntatic.wordpress.com/2007/05/18/ new-beginnings-with-obtiva/*.

Context

You have realized that you're not the first person to walk the path and that you are spending a lot of time exploring blind alleys.

Problem

You're walking along a path with no idea of what's around the next corner or how to prepare for it. You need help and guidance.

Solution

Seek out those who have gone ahead of you and strive to learn from them.

Ideally, you will find a master craftsman who will accept you as an apprentice. You will remain under her supervision throughout your apprenticeship, establishing your future on the foundation of your master's reputation. However, this ideal is exceptionally rare in today's world.

Our field is very young and therefore has few recognized masters. Furthermore, as an apprentice it can be difficult to tell who is truly a master craftsman. Therefore, it is more likely that your apprenticeship will be supervised by a series of mentors who possess varying degrees of mastery.

Real-world apprentices have to scratch and claw their way into the lives of master craftsmen and are grateful for whatever attention they can get, particularly face-to-face or, better yet, side-by-side. Having said that, you may find that the most influential and helpful mentors for you are not physically available. They may live in a different country; they may even be long dead, as in the case of someone like Edgar Dijkstra. But that doesn't mean that they can't still act as beacons, lighting the way forward.

> If you should end up with a teacher who doesn't seem right for you, first look inside. You might well be expecting more than any teacher can give.
>
> —George Leonard, *Mastery*, p. 71

When trying to Find Mentors, an apprentice must remember that we're all walking The Long Road and no one knows everything. It can be tempting to feel that your mentor must be a master because she knows so much more than you do. That temptation must be resisted, because you do not want to become so disillusioned with your mentor's inevitable weaknesses or blind spots that you feel you can no longer learn from someone who still has much to offer.

Dave finds a mentor

By the summer of 2002, I had been programming for less than two years and was starting to get glimpses of the vast difference between a beginner and a super-experienced practitioner. Reading Pete McBreen's *Software Craftsmanship* that summer compelled me to find a mentor. The book helped me see that if I wanted to become a great developer, I was going to have to reach out to more experienced developers and coordinate my own apprenticeship. I was at the height of Expanding My Bandwidth and had recently started attending ChAD, the Chicago Agile Developers user group. It was there that I (uncharacteristically) introduced myself to Wyatt Sutherland, the group's organizer. Immediately after finishing Pete's book, I emailed Wyatt and let him know that I was interested in being mentored. That was an uncomfortable email to send, but the payoff was huge. Wyatt responded by suggesting that we meet periodically for breakfast to talk about what we were working on. Over the following year, Wyatt became a great mentor to me. Although we never Rubbed Elbows, my relationship with someone like Wyatt, a highly regarded software consultant and world-class cellist (*http://yellowcello.com/yya/Wyatt.html*), was a huge confidence boost for an untrained, newbie programmer. Wyatt's mentoring was pivotal in my progress in agile software development, and propelled me to believe that I had the talent to join a development organization like ThoughtWorks.

While simple in concept and exceptionally important for your apprenticeship, finding people to guide you can be difficult. Sure, it's easy to locate authors, conference speakers, committers on popular open source projects, and developers of successful websites. But the difficulty is twofold. First, these people may not be interested in mentoring; and second, reaching out to ask for something as strange as "apprenticeship" can be incredibly intimidating. This is similar to the risks associated with diving into The Deep End. Just keep in mind that the risk of being rejected or thought strange by a potential mentor is low, while the potential payoff is huge. Even if the person is not interested in taking you on as a full-time apprentice, offering to take her out to lunch would be time and money well spent. If you are serious about achieving mastery, be tenacious about finding mentors to guide you. You would be hard-pressed to find any top-notch developers who cannot recall the powerful impact that their mentors had on them.

Your apprenticeship is unlikely to happen in isolation, and just as there will be people ahead of you, there will also be apprentices who have not yet reached your skill level. The other side of your search for mentors is that you must be willing to provide mentoring to those who seek it from you. Passing along what you have learned from your mentors is one of the ways in which you can begin the transition to journeyman status.

Action

Pick a tool, library, or community that has an active mailing list. Sign up to the list, but don't post any messages yet. Just lurk. Over time you will start to understand the values of the community and learn which of the subscribers are patient teachers. When you have this understanding, seek out the members of this list at the next conference and see if they would be interested in providing you with some informal advice about the lessons they have learned.

See Also

"The Deep End" (page 30) and "The Long Road" (page 38).

Kindred Spirits

Nothing is more powerful than a community of talented people working on related problems.

—Paul Graham, Hackers & Painters

Context

You are months or years into your apprenticeship and you find yourself discouraged by the culture of your development organization.

Problem

Organizational cultures that encourage software craftsmanship are rare. You find yourself stranded without mentors and in an atmosphere that seems at odds with your aspirations.

Solution

To keep your momentum going, especially in the absence of a full-time mentor, you need to be in frequent contact with people who are walking a similar road. Therefore you should seek out people like yourself who are also looking to excel.

The Long Road is not a road that anyone walks alone, and particularly during the years of your apprenticeship, you need camaraderie. This pattern is simple in principle, and for some people (our extroverted cohorts) it is simple in practice. For others, however, it can be difficult. Some relationships are brief but career-changing; others are long-lasting and help Nurture Your Passion. The following stories provide examples of the power of Kindred Spirits.

- Dave read *Extreme Programming Explained* in 2002 and dove headfirst into the XP and Agile community. He paid his own way to attend XP/Agile Universe 2002, which was conveniently hosted in a nearby suburb of Chicago. While at the conference, Dave met Roman, whom he had already been introduced to online through a local user group mailing list. Dave and Roman agreed to meet for lunch to discuss Joshua Kerievsky's book-in-progress *Refactoring to Patterns*. Roman worked at a large, multinational bank and Dave worked at an old, bloated nonprofit; not surprisingly, they both enjoyed the escape from the mediocrity of their respective development organizations and met every week for several years. They didn't end up discussing Joshua's book (because Dave first needed to read *Refactoring* and *Design Patterns*) but spent their time in all sorts of ways, discussing other books like *Peopleware*, learning Ruby on Dave's laptop, sharing horror stories, and offering each other solutions to the various problems they encountered over the years.

- Steve Tooke told us a story of meeting Shane in 2004 while working for a company in Manchester, England. Steve was an enthusiastic young programmer, and Shane was an experienced developer based in New Zealand. Although they were thousands of miles apart, their interactions were career-altering for Steve. Shane introduced him to books like *Design Patterns*, which gave them a shared language to describe the object-oriented designs they were working on together. The communication roadblocks of being separated by many time zones meant that Shane couldn't provide much direct mentoring, but for Steve, the connection itself and the knowledge that there was someone else in his development organization who was dedicated to excellence made a huge difference in his work.

Mentors are people who you want to emulate, and therefore can often feel a bit removed and sometimes intimidating. On the other hand, your community provides a safe environment for exploration and learning. Perhaps you are interested in advanced JavaScript, and one of your Kindred Spirits is investigating Haskell. You can feel free to show each other what you're learning and have no obligation to follow the other's lead. This is different from a mentor-based relationship, where the apprentice might feel obliged to drop his interest in JavaScript and pursue Haskell simply because the mentor sees it as a superior language, disregarding the fact that the apprentice needs to learn JavaScript for his current project. Keep this in mind and complement the Find Mentors pattern with a community of Kindred Spirits with whom you can let down your guard.

Despite the many benefits of a community of like-minded folk, you must also be aware of group-think. Force yourself to retain the capacity to ask questions that shock your community. Try to use that little bit of intellectual distance to generate the kind of respectful dissent that will keep your community healthy. Your community's health can be measured in the way it reacts to new ideas. Does it embrace the idea after vigorous debate and experimentation? Or does it quickly reject the idea and the person who proposed it? Today's dissident is tomorrow's leader, and one of the most valuable services you can provide to your community is defending it against those who believe that marching in lockstep is the price of membership.

Action

List all the communities you could potentially join based on the tools you use, the languages you know, the people you have worked with, the blogs you read, and the ideas you are intrigued by. Identify which of those groups gather in the real world in your city. One by one, attend all these gatherings, and decide which groups seem most interesting.

What if none of the groups regularly meet near you? In that case, you've just been given a golden opportunity to create one of these gatherings. Start a regular meetup of software craftsmen in your region. It's a lot less work than you would think. Just don't make the mistake of restricting the membership or the topics too early. Instead, advertise anywhere and everywhere that software developers in your region might see it.

As your group grows, feel free to explore a wide and bizarre range of topics until you have a core group of irregulars. Over time, that self-selected group of irregulars will define the nature of your group. You won't always have the same people attending every fortnight—that's what makes them irregulars. Groups like the Extreme Tuesday Club have a few hundred "members"; on any given Tuesday there will only be a dozen or so people in attendance. If your group becomes large enough and energetic enough, it will sustain itself even when you are not there. That's when you know you have a community.

See Also

"Find Mentors" (page 61), "Nurture Your Passion" (page 45), and "The Long Road" (page 38).

Rubbing Elbows

I enjoy being given a certain amount of freedom in order to interpret or to come up with stuff, but I do enjoy collaboration. I seek and thrive on projects where I am going to learn from the people I'm working with.

—William Kempe

Context

While you may have mentors and kindred spirits that you meet with periodically, when it comes to developing software, you work alone.

Problem

Your productivity has reached a plateau, your learning is stagnating, and you have the feeling that there are superior techniques and approaches to the craft that are eluding you.

Solution

Find ways to sit with another software developer and accomplish a hands-on task together, side-by-side. There are some things that can only be learned while you are sitting with another software developer to accomplish a shared objective.

This pattern can be closely related to Kindred Spirits. This was the case for Dave, who found an ally in Roman and then literally rubbed elbows over lunch as they learned together about technologies like the Ruby programming language and Eclipse plug-in development. Yet, even if Roman had not been a kindred spirit, Dave would still have benefited by working side-by-side with a talented programmer, even on pet projects. There will always be certain micro-techniques that you will only learn when collaborating closely with a colleague. These are usually seen as too trivial to mention when teaching, but their impact adds up. Collaborating with Roman was critical for Dave's progress as a developer, since he rarely had the opportunity to work with talented developers at that time in his career.

The development practice of Pair Programming is a concrete example of this pattern, and apprentices should look for opportunities to work on teams that use this technique. While pair programming can be an excellent technique for learning, it is a complex activity and is not always an inherently positive experience. However, when used effectively, it is one of the most powerful ways to learn, particularly from mentors. So how do you know if pair programming is being used effectively? And what can an apprentice do about it?

You will often feel lost or far behind your counterpart when you're implementing this pattern via pair programming. This does not mean pair programming is failing—it simply means you need to either slow things down by asking questions or endure the feeling of being lost and try to pick up the bits that you do understand. But if you feel chronically behind, week after week, and you're beginning to despair, then it's time to make a change. You may be stuck with a poor pair programming partner, or your partner may need some suggestions to improve your experience. As an apprentice, you may not have much power to change your situation, but if you're on a project with more than a few people, you can likely find an opportunity to alternate days or weeks between pair programming partners. This rotation may help jiggle you out of your troublesome situation and get you back on the path of progress. Additionally, if you're practicing test-driven development, you can suggest Ping-Pong Programming[||] as a way to increase your participation.

According to Richard Sennett's *The Craftsman*, the ideal craft workshop is a place for "absorption into tacit knowledge, unspoken and uncodified in words" of the "thousand little everyday moves that add up in sum to a practice" (p. 77). Since such ideal environments are now so rare, we have to use the Rubbing Elbows pattern as a modern-day substitute. The applications of this pattern are not limited merely to pair programming. The goal is to find ways to expose yourself to the daily working habits of other skilled people, and observe the ways in which they gradually refine those habits into even greater skill. These habits extend beyond coding and into all aspects of software development.

For instance, you might collaborate with someone on an academic paper or a presentation or at an open source project's sprint. Or, as happened to Ade, you might find yourself volunteering to help somebody who wants to apply graph theory to design the dependency management

[||] Dave Hoover, "Ping-Pong Programming." Available at: *http://www.stickyminds.com/s.asp?F=S9101_COL_2.*

component of a content management system written in Unix shell script! Sharing a whiteboard with someone who wants to use a very low-level tool to solve a problem you would automatically solve with a high-level language (or vice versa) forces you to temporarily think like that other person in order to communicate effectively. Even if you ultimately reject that viewpoint, you have gained a new way of looking at problems. That perspective may be just the right solution to some future problem, even if in the short term you find it jarring.

Whether your experience rubbing elbows is positive or negative, you should Record What You Learn so that you can reflect on your experiences later on. Someday you will likely be in the same position as your pair programming partner, and your past experiences will give you precious insight into the mindset of the junior person sitting next to you.

Action

Find someone you know who has already expressed an interest in starting or contributing to an open source project. Arrange to spend one evening a week working together on the project. See how long the two of you can keep each other motivated. The strains of a busy life will inevitably weaken the motivation behind your collaboration; when that happens, you must adapt and find ways to keep the project going until that motivation returns. Of course, if motivation never returns, it is up to you to seek out a new partnership where you can learn new things.

See Also

"Kindred Spirits" (page 64) and "Record What You Learn" (page 88).

Sweep the Floor

> **In the craft tradition, newcomers start as apprentices to a master craftsman. They start by contributing to the simpler tasks, and as they learn and become more skilled, they slowly graduate to larger, more complex tasks.**
>
> —*Pete McBreen, Software Craftsmanship*

Context

You are a new apprentice on a project.

Problem

You're unsure of your place on the team, and the team is unsure of you. You wish to find a means of contributing to the team's work, earning the team's trust, and growing in stature as a craftsman.

Solution

Volunteer for simple, unglamorous, yet necessary, tasks. This is a good way to contribute to the team's success early on by showing that you can do a high-quality job even when it doesn't seem to matter. Of course, skimping on quality in the unglamorous portions of any project often leads to trouble later on, when it turns out that the unglamorous parts of the project are vitally important.

Paul literally sweeps the floor

I had the privilege to be trained in a formal software apprenticeship environment. Object Mentor hired me when I was seventeen and brought me back every summer and winter break during college. When I started my apprenticeship, I did not know how to write software. I had written some code to create simple programs and scripts for fun. When I started my software apprenticeship out, there were few places I could provide value to the company's business. I could not write software and could obviously not teach others how to write software.

At the time, Object Mentor employed many of the successful eXtreme Programming leaders to teach a course about XP. As the star-struck young apprentice, I was commissioned to build the perfect pair programming tables they had designed. Also, I would put together the computers, install the correct software for the exercises, and clean up the room. These tasks helped me to build confidence in being part of the team, part of the company. As I struggled learning to write code, I could still contribute with specific talents and tasks that needed less skill.

Slowly, as my apprenticeship progressed, I would take on more technically challenging assignments. However, they were still often the ones you would assign to the low man on the totem pole. Tasks like moving servers, figuring out the backup systems, and updating content on the website. These tasks were helpful for me to get small victories at a time when it was hard to get those victories writing code.

Playing the role of a traditional apprentice also helped me to build up humility and respect for the senior craftsmen. I remember Uncle Bob Martin came into a room, saw the trash overflowing, and changed the garbage bag. My mentor scolded me and appropriately said that it is not the job of the master craftsman to take out the garbage. It is a sign of respect and piety that was an important lesson for me to learn.

—Paul Pagel, email

Unlike Paul, most apprentices won't literally be sweeping the floor. However, the tasks you volunteer for will matter just as much to the ongoing health of the team.

Examples of these tasks include maintaining the build system, production support, responding to maintenance requests, bug fixing, code review, eliminating technical debt, setting up the project wiki, updating documentation, acting as a sounding board for other people's ideas, and so on. Typically, you'll want to focus on the edges of the system where there is less risk, rather than the core where there are usually many dependencies and lots of complexity. Jean Lave and Etienne Wenger observed apprentices in diverse industries and found that "a newcomer's tasks tend to be positioned at the ends of the branches of work processes, rather than in the middle of linked work segments" (*Situated Learning*, p. 110). These sorts of fringe tasks benefit the team, but they will also benefit you as an apprentice, because such chores are often skipped in academic courses and by doing them you can fill in the gaps in your knowledge. This experience will serve you well as a journeyman too, because any master who takes you on will understand how valuable it is to have someone to do the unglamorous work. After all, if no one sweeps the floor, then the glamorous work can't be done because the team is hip-deep in dirt.

Of course, Sweeping the Floor can be tough to swallow if you have spent a lot of time and money on a computer science education. In theory, you've already paid your dues by pulling frequent all-night debugging sessions and enduring countless menial assignments from your professors. Unfortunately, in the workplace your education is worth less than you might think. Sure, there are plenty of organizations that make a computer science degree a high priority when they're hiring people, but getting hired is different from joining a team. Once you're in the door, all that education is doing for you is raising people's expectations about what you'll deliver on your first day (and hopefully it prepared you for that first day!). The same can be said if you are a self-taught person who "paid your dues" on previous projects. Regardless of where you came from, when you join a new project you are starting from square one. You should take this opportunity to send a message to the team that you *want* to contribute, even if it means taking on unsexy tasks.

There are a few negative consequences that may occur when you apply this pattern. One is that you may end up as the team's gopher, condemned to do the menial tasks no one else will do. And while you're unlikely to be seen as overstepping your boundaries due to the unglamorous nature of the tasks you've chosen there is a danger that you may not be able to turn your early success into a case for being given more challenging assignments. Alternatively, you may find yourself intimidated by doing anything other than Sweeping the Floor. There is also the danger that you may not be able to develop an appreciation for the bigger picture if you only work on piecemeal tasks with no wider coherence. If you find yourself in any of these situations, try to Nurture Your Passion, Unleash Your Enthusiasm, advocate for yourself, and look for every opportunity to prove yourself worthy of higher-level work.

Action

What's the grungiest task that your team has been putting off for months? It will be the one that everybody complains about and that no one wants to tackle. Tackle it. And don't just hold your nose and force yourself to do it; see if you can creatively resolve the problem in a way that exceeds people's expectations and makes it fun for you.

See Also

"Nurture Your Passion" (page 45) and "Unleash Your Enthusiasm" (page 22).

Wrapping Up

Humility is one of the foundations of a successful apprenticeship. Combined with ambition, humility will help keep you focused and progressing in the right direction. Without it, you're susceptible to prematurely declaring your apprenticeship complete and missing out on some important lessons. Perhaps you feel proud of a significant project or subsystem you've delivered and you believe that it proves that you have become a journeyman. Perhaps. But have you delivered something significant on more than one platform? How much more would you learn if you tried your hand at a different language? Any ambitious apprentice's natural instinct will be to try to race to the finish line, to become a journeyman as quickly as possible. Remember, though, that you are walking The Long Road, and this journey is not a sprint. Take the time to get the most out of your apprenticeship, and understand that whether you have been programming for three months or five years, you are still very much a beginner when it comes to software craftsmanship.

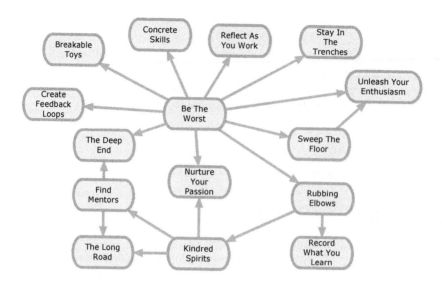

CHAPTER FIVE

Perpetual Learning

If we let ourselves, we shall always be waiting for some distraction or other to end before we can really get down to our work. The only people who achieve much are those who want knowledge so badly that they seek it while the conditions are still unfavourable. Favourable conditions never come.

—C.S. Lewis, "Learning in War-Time", *The Weight of Glory and Other Addresses*

Andy Hunt, a highly respected software craftsman, has asserted numerous times that software development is composed of two primary activities: learning and communication (*Pragmatic Thinking and Learning*, p. 3). We would build on that idea and assert that the core theme of an apprenticeship is learning and the dominant trait of a successful apprentice is a demonstration of her learning abilities. Apprentices are thirsty for opportunities to replace their ignorance with skill. This is no small feat when faced with the complexities of our work and the seemingly overwhelming amount of information that an apprentice must deal with. Beyond the fundamental act of learning Concrete Skills, an apprentice must also learn how to learn, for the transition to journeyman will certainly not remove the need for learning. One trait of a master craftsman is a willingness to set aside hard-won expertise in a specific domain in order to learn something new. Learning is a perpetual activity for those on The Long Road to mastery.

The Perpetual Learning patterns are applicable for your entire career, but with the apprentice's emphasis on learning, it is critical that these patterns be applied early on in your journey. Expanding Your Bandwidth is the fundamental activity for apprentices looking to accelerate growth and facilitates several of the other Perpetual Learning patterns, such as Breakable Toys; Use the Source; and Practice, Practice, Practice. All three of these patterns grow out of an exposure to new information or a desire to acquire new knowledge: whether you're practicing a new technique, building something in an effort to learn a new platform, or studying the source code of an innovative new open source tool. These more concrete patterns are followed by the softer self-discovery patterns that proceed from Reflect as You Work, which leads to Recording and Sharing what you're learning. The critical patterns to take with you into the years beyond apprenticeship are Create Feedback Loops and Learn How You Fail. To transition to journeyman and ultimately master craftsman, you are going to need to be skilled at creating feedback loops, and also to be intimately familiar with your weaknesses.

Expand Your Bandwidth

[L]earning about what we don't know is often more important than doing things we already know how to do.

—Jim Highsmith, *Agile Software Development Ecosystems*

Context

You have picked up a basic set of skills.

Problem

Your understanding of software development is narrow and focused only on the low-level details of what you've worked on in your day job.

Solution

You have been drinking steadily through a straw. But there are seasons in an apprenticeship when one must drink from the fire hose of information available to most software developers.

Expanding your ability to take in new information is a critical, though sometimes overwhelming, step for apprentices. You must develop the discipline and techniques necessary to efficiently absorb new information, as well as to understand it, retain it, and apply it. This pattern means more than reading a book about an unfamiliar aspect of software development. It involves seeking out new knowledge and experiences in multiple dimensions. For example:

- Sign up for Google Reader (or another blog aggregator) and begin subscribing to software development blogs. With modern machine translation technologies, you don't even have to restrict yourself to those who write in English. You can follow Tim O'Reilly's advice and track the blogs of what he calls "alpha geeks" across a variety of technology domains.[*] These people aren't necessarily the best programmers, but collectively they tend to sense new trends years before the rest of us. Consider using your own blog to reflect on the themes you pick up from these bloggers.

- Start following some software luminaries on Twitter and pay attention to what they're working on.

- Subscribe to a moderately high-traffic online mailing list and try to answer people's questions by reproducing their issues.

- Join a newly formed local user group that is excited about a new technology. Don't just attend silently—introduce yourself to the organizer and offer to help.

- Persuade your employer to send you to a technical conference. Even if they won't pay for you to attend, you can still read the slides on the website and download audio/video of the speeches.

- After you read a book, contact the author with a note of appreciation and a question. Authors, speakers, and luminaries may seem intimidating or busy, but they often enjoy corresponding with readers.

- Don't forget that there are hundreds of online academic courses, podcasts, and videos (such as Google's extensive series of Tech Talks) available for free through iTunes and YouTube.

As the priorities of your apprenticeship shift, you will eventually need to turn off the fire hose so that you can focus on project work. But there should be at least one season during your apprenticeship during which you use this pattern. It's important not just because of the knowledge you will pick up during this time, but because it is actually a skill to be developed in and of itself. Journeymen and masters seek out opportunities where this pattern can be used

---

[*] Tim O'Reilly, "Watching the 'Alpha Geeks': OS X and the Next Big Thing." Available at: *http://www .linuxdevcenter.com/pub/a/mac/2002/05/14/oreilly_wwdc_keynote.html*.

to advance their careers and craftsmanship, particularly when they want to get into a new technology.

Dave and the firehose

When I was given the opportunity to learn Perl by my employer in late 2000, I began expanding my bandwidth immediately. I felt like I had a lot of catching up to do, so after I read a couple Perl books, I looked for any possible opportunity to learn more. I was determined to reach the next level as a Perl developer as quickly as possible, and knew that just taking one book at a time wasn't going to be fast enough (I'm competitive, OK?). So I joined *http://perlmonks.org*, asked and answered questions on comp.lang.perl.misc (*http://groups.google.com/group/comp.lang.perl .misc*), attended a couple Perl Mongers (*http://pm.org/*) meetings, and started playing Perl Golf (yes, competitively). After about a year of this, I had to scale down my intake for the sake of my sanity and my marriage. But I had made progress, and had many more resources at my disposal when I found myself stumped.

Then, in the spring of 2002, I read Kent Beck's *Extreme Programming Explained* and saw an opportunity to grow beyond Perl into the world of test-driven development, pair programming, object-oriented design, and design patterns. Once again I expanded my bandwidth and read a pile of excellent books, started attending a local agile software development user group, paid my way to an XP/Agile Universe conference (thankfully held near my home that year), participated on the extreme programming mailing list, started reading relevant blogs, and subsequently started blogging (*http://www.redsquirrel.com/blog/archives/00000004.html*). The outcome of this season of expanding my bandwidth won me a job at ThoughtWorks, a transnational agile consulting company. My career and apprenticeship were forever changed by the learning opportunities that ThoughtWorks gave me.

As I transitioned from apprentice to journeyman toward the end of 2005, I saw another opportunity on the horizon: Ruby on Rails was on the rise. This allowed me to join Obtiva, a local consulting company that better fit my lifestyle, where I founded Obtiva's Software Studio and kick-started Obtiva's apprenticeship program.

Once you understand *how* to Expand Your Bandwidth, the next step is to understand *when* to Expand Your Bandwidth. It's possible to become obsessed with gathering and consuming new information, particularly as it becomes easier and easier to get at up-to-the-second thoughts on the most prolific thinkers in our industry. Some people could become lost in the sea of interesting information, and never come back to actually crafting software. While Expanding Your Bandwidth can be fun and is an interesting skill in and of itself, for the apprentice it is a means to an end. Use this pattern judiciously, for while it will accelerate your learning, it will slow down your development velocity, and therefore will have diminishing returns if applied for more than a few months.

Action

Attend a local user group within the next month. Research a related national conference you'd like to attend. Start reading a book by one of the conference speakers. Contact the author with some questions after you're finished with the book.

Practice, Practice, Practice

The people we know as masters don't devote themselves to their particular skill just to get better at it. The truth is, they love to practice—and because of this they do get better. And then to complete the circle, the better they get the more they enjoy performing the basic moves over and over again.

—George Leonard, Mastery

Context

You want to get better at the things you do and you want to develop Concrete Skills in new areas.

Problem

The performance of your daily programming activities does not give you room to learn by making mistakes. It's as if you're always on stage.

Solution

Take the time to practice your craft without interruptions, in an environment where you can feel comfortable making mistakes.

In an ideal world we would use the technique of "deliberate practice" as described in K. Anders Ericsson's research, and a mentor would assign you an exercise based on her understanding of your strengths and weaknesses. When you finished the exercise, the mentor would work with you to rate your performance using an objective metric and then work with you to devise the next exercise. Your mentor then would use her experience of teaching other students to devise new and more challenging exercises that would encourage you to reflect on your skills, find more effective work habits, and develop the ability to "see" in terms of ever more abstract "chunks" of knowledge. Over time, this chain of exercises would hone your strengths and correct your weaknesses. Sadly we do not live in an ideal world, and apprentices must fall back on their own resources to achieve the same effect.

In software we do our practicing on the job, and that's why we make mistakes on the job. We need to find ways of splitting the practice from the profession. We need practice sessions.

—Dave Thomas[†]

"Pragmatic" Dave Thomas borrowed the concept of code katas from martial arts. A kata is a choreographed sequence of movements provided by a master to help his students internalize the fundamentals of the art. Katas are performed without opponents, emphasizing fluidity, power, speed, and control. Dave Thomas posted kata in his blog, encouraging craftsmen to use the kata to practice.

Laurent Bossavit and a group of software developers in Paris took the martial arts metaphor a step further and created a coder's dojo, a place where people could meet regularly to publicly perform code katas. "Uncle" Bob Martin, inspired by the Paris dojo, also posts katas to his blog, espousing the merits of practicing the craft:

> Beginners learn by *doing*, not through lecture. They practice, and practice, and practice.... By repeating and repeating these same exercises, we sharpen our skills, we train our bodies and our minds to respond to the disciplines of TDD and simple design. We wire, and rewire, and rewire, and rewire our neurons to react in the right way.

—Robert Martin[‡]

Obviously code kata are just one of the ways to Practice, Practice, Practice (Breakable Toys are another). The key to this pattern is to carve out some time to develop software in a stress-free and playful environment: no release dates, no production issues, no interruptions. As Dave Thomas says of practicing, "It has to be acceptable to relax, because if you aren't relaxed you're not going to learn from the practice."

Short feedback loops need to be incorporated into your practice sessions. While practice is good in theory, if you're not getting periodic feedback you're probably developing bad habits. This is the beauty of the coder's dojo: public performance within the context of a tight-knit community of craftsmen. This need for constant feedback lessens as you grow as a craftsman, and is gradually replaced by your duty to take on the role of a senior apprentice, modeling good habits by practicing with less experienced developers.

One of the reasons that the masters described by George Leonard love to practice is that they do something a little bit different each time an exercise is performed. The point is not to hone your memory, but to discover the nuances in even the simplest skilled activity. Your grandmother may have told you that practice makes perfect. She was wrong. In fact, practice makes permanent. So be careful what you practice, and constantly evaluate it to ensure you haven't gone stale. Choosing the right thing to practice every day is a skill almost as important as the act of repeated practice. A good way to ensure you have interesting exercises to use in

---

† Dave Thomas on Code Kata: *http://codekata.pragprog.com/2007/01/code_kata_backg.html*.

‡ Robert Martin on the Programming Dojo: *http://butunclebob.com/ArticleS.UncleBob .TheProgrammingDojo*.

your practice sessions is to trawl through old books like *Programming Pearls, More Programming Pearls,* or *Etudes for Programmers.* They were written long enough ago that they had no choice but to focus on the fundamentals of computer science rather than the latest fashionable framework. Their authors understood that getting the fundamentals of algorithmic complexity and data structures deeply ingrained is seldom harmful and rarely stops being useful. These topics also offer a near-infinite source of interesting little problems to keep your practice sessions interesting, fresh, and educational.

Action

Find an exercise in one of the previously mentioned books or contrive one of your own. Make sure that it's just a little harder than one you know you can easily solve. You should have to struggle to solve it the first time. Solve this exercise from scratch once a week for the next four weeks, and observe how your solutions evolve. What does this tell you about your strengths and weaknesses as a programmer? Take that knowledge and try to find or devise a new exercise that will have a measurable impact on your abilities. Repeat.

See Also

"Breakable Toys" (page 79) and "Concrete Skills" (page 24).

Breakable Toys

> You can't do anything really well unless you love it, and if you love to hack you'll inevitably be working on projects of your own.
>
> —*Paul Graham, Hackers & Painters*

> We can all benefit by doing occasional "toy" programs, when artificial restrictions are set up, so that we are forced to push our abilities to the limit.
>
> —*Donald Knuth, The Art of Computer Programming*

Context

Experience is built upon failure as much as (if not more than) success.

Problem

You work in an environment that does not allow for failure. Yet failure is often the best way to learn anything. Only by attempting to do bold things, failing, learning from that failure, and trying again do we grow into the kind of people who can succeed when faced with difficult problems.

Solution

Budget for failure by designing and building toy systems that are similar in toolset, but not in scope to the systems you build at work.

If experience is built upon failure as much as success, then you need a more or less private space where you can seek out failure. In juggling, the three-ball juggler who never attempts five balls never makes the step up. Yet the one who gets backaches from having to pick up dropped balls for hours on end will eventually get it right. The same lesson applies to software. Just as the three-ball juggler would not attempt to juggle five balls during a performance, software developers need a safe place to make mistakes.

As a teenager working in Nova Scotia, Steve Baker was looked upon as a leader and an expert within his small development organization. Steve described how these expectations impacted him: "Everyone expected me to already know the right way to do it. Since I couldn't use those projects as a learning experience, I had to stop learning." This was similar to Ade's consulting experiences, where he couldn't afford to be wrong and he couldn't just walk away from people who were depending on him to always be right. Ade knew that in order to learn, he needed the freedom to drop the ball. Like countless software developers before him, Ade used Breakable Toys to help him learn.

When implementing the Breakable Toys pattern, make your systems relevant and useful to your life as an apprentice. For example, build your own wiki, calendar, or address book. Your solutions might be massively overengineered for the problem they're solving, and probably could easily be replaced by something off the shelf. However, these projects are where you are allowed to fail. They're the projects where you can try ideas and techniques that might lead to catastrophic failure. But the only one who can be hurt by their failure is you.

A classic example of the use of this pattern is the multitude of people who have built their own wikis. A personal wiki is a great tool for the apprentice because you can use it to Record What You Learn. Wikis make good Breakable Toys because they can be incredibly simple§ and you can Use the Source to find countless examples to look. Over time, maintaining a wiki can teach you about HTTP, REST, parsing, web design, caching, full-text search, databases, and concurrency. If you stick with it long enough, it will also teach you about data migration when

---

§ Shortest Wiki Contest: *http://c2.com/cgi/wiki?ShortestWikiContest*.

you eventually add a feature that requires a different storage format and you don't want to throw away all your data.

Other examples of Breakable Toys include games like Tetris and Tic-Tac-Toe (one of our ex-colleagues is in the habit of writing a game in every new language he learns), blogging software, and IRC clients. The essential point is that building the toy involves learning new things, giving you an opportunity to gain a deeper understanding of your tools in an environment that is both safe (since you are the only or most important user) and where there is still room for you to better serve your own needs as a user than even the slickest of commercial alternatives.

These are *your* Breakable Toys. As you carry them with you from job to job, some of them will become living embodiments of your craftsmanship. Despite that, remember that they're toys and as such should be fun. If they're not fun, then after the initial burst of enthusiasm they will gather dust while you focus your energies on the things you actually enjoy building.

Often these toys are simple reimplementations of industry-standard tools that give you a deeper understanding of the forces that led to the current design of that tool. There's even the possibility that one of your toys will take on a life of its own and acquire other users. In those cases you may find yourself having to seek out a new breakable toy.

Linus builds a toy OS[ǁ]

```
From: torvalds@klaava.Helsinki.FI (Linus Benedict Torvalds)
Newsgroups: comp.os.minix
Subject: What would you like to see most in minix?
Summary: small poll for my new operating system
Message-ID: <1991Aug25.205708.9541@klaava.Helsinki.FI>
Date: 25 Aug 91 20:57:08 GMT
Organization: University of Helsinki

Hello everybody out there using minix -

I'm doing a (free) operating system (just a hobby, won't be big and
professional like gnu) for 386(486) AT clones.  This has been brewing
since april, and is starting to get ready.  I'd like any feedback on
things people like/dislike in minix, as my OS resembles it somewhat
(same physical layout of the file-system (due to practical reasons)
among other things).

I've currently ported bash(1.08) and gcc(1.40), and things seem to work.
This implies that I'll get something practical within a few months, and
I'd like to know what features most people would want.  Any suggestions
are welcome, but I won't promise I'll implement them :-)

            Linus (torvalds@kruuna.helsinki.fi)

PS.  Yes - it's free of any minix code, and it has a multi-threaded fs.
```

ǁ The first public announcement of Linux *http://groups.google.com/group/comp.os.minix/browse_thread/thread/ 76536d1fb451ac60/b813d52cbc5a044b.*

```
It is NOT protable (uses 386 task switching etc), and it probably never
will support anything other than AT-harddisks, as that's all I have :-(.
```

The Breakable Toys pattern is similar to Be the Worst, but that pattern is about finding a team where you can grow. Breakable Toys is more about deliberately creating opportunities to learn by stepping beyond your boundaries and single-handedly building complete software projects. It is also related to The White Belt and Confront Your Ignorance, but is less focused on letting go of your previous knowledge.

Action

Use your favorite tools to build the world's simplest wiki while still maintaining the highest standards of quality. The initial version doesn't need to have anything more than a simple user interface that lets you view and edit plain-text files. Over time, you can add more features and find interesting ways to distinguish your wiki from the thousands that already exist. Do not be constrained by existing implementations; instead, let your professional interests guide you. For instance, you might have an interest in search engines; in this case your wiki could experiment with ranking algorithms or tagging. It really doesn't matter what you decide to do, as long as you experiment and learn.

See Also

"Be the Worst" (page 58), "Confront Your Ignorance" (page 28), "Record What You Learn" (page 88), and "Use the Source" (page 82).

Use the Source

> **The best way to prepare [to be a programmer] is to write programs, and to study great programs that other people have written. In my case, I went to the garbage cans at the Computer Science Center and fished out listings of their operating system.**
>
> —Bill Gates, Programmers at Work

Context

Newcomers to the open source world often find that their questions are answered with the phrase "Use the source, Luke." This expresses a fundamental truth about software: the code is the ultimate arbiter. The programmer's intentions are irrelevant if the code disagrees. Only by reading the code can one truly understand a system.

Problem

Without exemplars of good practice to study and emulate, the Practice, Practice, Practice pattern only entrenches the bad habits you don't know you have. If you never walk a mile in someone else's moccasins, you may come to believe that all shoes are meant to have stones in them. So how do you find out if your work is any good, given that those around you may not have the ability to tell good code from bad?

Solution

Seek out other people's code and read it. Start with the applications and tools you use every day. As an apprentice, one of the beliefs that can hold you back is the idea that the people who built the tools that you depend on are somehow different or special or better than you are. By reading their code you can learn to program like them, and more importantly, you can start to understand the thought processes that created the infrastructure that surrounds you.

When examining an open source project, get in the habit of downloading the current version of the source code (preferably from its source control system) so that you can inspect its history and track future progress. Examine the structure of the codebase and try to work out why the files were laid out that way. See if there is a rationale behind the way the developers modularized the codebase and compare it to the way you would have done it.

Try to refactor the codebases in order to understand why the programmers made the choices they did, and to see what the consequences would have been if you had been the one writing the code. This doesn't just give you a better understanding of these projects; it also ensures that you can build the projects. And if you find a better way to do something, you are in a good position to contribute.

As you work through the codebase, you will inevitably come across decisions that you passionately disagree with. Ask yourself if perhaps the developers knew something you don't or vice versa. Consider the possibility that this was a legacy design that needs to be refactored away, and think about whether putting together a toy implementation of the feature might be educational.

In addition to reading other people's code (and, where requested, providing feedback), try to find people around you who are interested in reading your source code. If you can learn to embrace their feedback while filtering out personal idiosyncrasies, you will become a better programmer. And remember, to become a journeyman you have to help others grow, so be open to reading other people's source code as well.

A common approach among the programmers we interviewed involves joining a team or project that uses code reviews or pair programming. These practices create environments in which the programmers could safely spend time reading other people's code, having others read their code, and learning from each other. These groups tend to produce extremely strong programmers. Other environments, such as most academic computer science departments, tend to overlook the fact that working programmers spend far more time reading code than writing code. They take this approach because making every student reinvent the wheel creates artifacts that are easy to grade. However, training yourself to be better at the task that takes up most of your working day is an optimization that yields greater rewards in the long run. This is true even if the nonprogrammers who are often in charge of these environments don't appreciate it.

By reading a wide variety of good, bad, and indifferent code written by other people you can start to learn about the idioms and subtleties of your particular language community. Over time, this will develop your ability to divine people's intentions from the code they have written. It will also help you learn to deal with those occasions when the two have diverged. These skills will make you a more valuable part of a team, because you'll be able to work on other people's code without always having to rewrite it because you can't tell what it does.

Eventually you'll acquire a toolbox of tricks and subtleties gleaned from other people's code. This hones your ability to solve small problems quickly and easily, just because you've seen something similar before. You'll be able to tackle problems that others consider impossible because they don't have access to your toolbox.

Take a look at Linus Torvalds's code for the Git distributed source control system or anything written by Daniel J. Bernstein (commonly known as djb). Programmers like Linus and djb casually use data structures and algorithms most of us have never even heard about. They're not magicians—they have merely spent time building a bigger and better toolbox than most people. The advantage of open source is that their toolboxes are open for you to inspect, and you can make their tools your own.

One of the problems with the field of software development is the lack of teachers. But thanks to the proliferation of open source projects on sites like sourceforge.net, GitHub, and Google Code, you can learn from a more or less representative sample of the global community of programmers. Unlike in traditional teaching, these are not toy projects designed to illustrate a point, rife with shortcuts and "exercises for the reader" when things get difficult. These are real projects that solve real problems and are constantly in flux. You can track a project as its developers learn and adapt to new requirements. By studying the way real codebases evolve, you can better appreciate the effects of design decisions without having to build hundreds of software projects yourself. This offers an opportunity to learn from other people's mistakes and to acquire a more vital skill than mere code reading: the ability to learn without being taught.

In *Programmers at Work*, Bill Gates said that "one of the finest tests of programming ability is to hand the programmer about 30 pages of code and see how quickly he can read through and understand it." He had realized something important. People who can quickly absorb knowledge directly from the code soon become much better programmers, because their teacher is every line of code written by every programmer ever born.

The best way to learn about patterns, idioms, and best practices is to read open source code. See how other people are doing it. It's a great way to stay current, and it's free.

—Chris Wanstrath in Keynote at Ruby Hoedown 2008[#]

Action

Pick an algorithmically sophisticated open source project such as a source control—system, for example, Subversion, Git, or Mercurial. Browse the project's source, noting down the algorithms, data structures, and design ideas that are new to you. Now write a blog post describing the architecture of the project and emphasizing the new ideas you have learned. Do you see places in your everyday work where the same ideas can be applied?

See Also

"Practice, Practice, Practice" (page 77).

Reflect As You Work

**Self-examination is hard, but I believe we can learn more
from studying our failures than from our successes.**

—Norm Kerth, Project Retrospectives

Context

Anyone who is reasonably competent will find themselves being pushed up the promotion ladder over the years. Sooner or later you end up wearing the senior developer hat in a corporate team or open source project. If you do not take steps to prepare yourself for that elevation, you may suddenly find yourself a victim of the Peter Principle, where you are promoted to your "level of incompetence."

Problem

As the number of years and projects you have under your belt increases, you find yourself awaiting the epiphany that will magically make you "experienced."

[#] Keynote at Ruby Hoedown 2008. Video at *http://rubyhoedown2008.confreaks.com/08-chris-wanstrath -keynote.html*. Transcript at *http://gist.github.com/6443*.

Solution

Become a reflective practitioner of software development. This involves regular introspection into how you are working. Consider whether your practices are novel, innovative, or outdated. Ask yourself questions about the things that the rest of your team takes for granted. If there is something particularly painful or pleasant about your current work, ask yourself how it got that way, and if things are negative, how can they be improved? The goal is to extract the maximum amount of educational value from every experience by taking it apart and putting it back together in new and interesting ways.

One technique that's useful in making this kind of reflection explicit is to use something like a Personal Practices Map. This is an idea that Joe Walnes introduced at London's Extreme Tuesday Club. It involves people consciously writing down the things they do and the connections between them. After everybody has written down their practices, the group discusses the practices that have been identified. If you take a look at the web page "Maps of People's Personal Practices," * you will see maps created by Ade and several other developers.

One of the consequences of repeatedly using this technique is that it highlights the changes in your set of practices. So for example, in the years since 2003, Ade has moved from "never using debuggers" to practicing "test-driven debugging" to starting to deliberately use invariants when implementing complex algorithms. The existence of a tangible and visible map of your practices leads to deeper reflection about the effect of any one change in the techniques you use. In Ade's case, the adoption of test-driven development led to the reevaluation of all the other practices, and the map became a tool for visualizing this change.

This process of observation, reflection, and change isn't limited to just your own activities. Unobtrusively watch the journeymen and master craftsmen on your team. Reflect on the practices, processes, and techniques they use to see if they can be connected to other parts of your experience. Even as an apprentice, you can discover novel ideas simply by closely observing more experienced craftsmen as they go about their work.

In 2004, Dave was part of an XP team that contained several world-class developers. They had a fairly standard style of pair programming: one guy would write a test and slid the keyboard over to his pair, and his pair would make the test pass, immediately write a test, and slide the keyboard back to the first guy. The first guy would pass the test and so on. This style of pair programming was never really discussed; it just emerged out of their respective experiences.

Dave joined his next project, and while explaining this style of pair programming to his new teammates he realized that the style needed a name. Dave blogged about it, which kicked off a chain reaction that quickly led to an offer to write a few columns for StickyMinds.com. All this happened simply because Dave reflected on the practices introduced by more senior developers.

---

* *http://www.xpdeveloper.net/xpdwiki/Wiki.jsp?page=MapsOfPeoplesPersonalPractices*

The Agile community has adopted a version of this process. Driven by Norm Kerth's book *Project Retrospectives*, it involves the team periodically gathering to look back on the state of the project in order to find ways to improve. As such, it is more formal than the continual self-analysis that an apprentice will undertake. It also requires reasonably enlightened management willing to provide a safe environment by honoring Kerth's prime directive: "Regardless of what we discover, we understand and truly believe that everyone did the best job they could, given what they knew at the time, their skills and abilities, the resources available, and the situation at hand."[†]

Apprentices won't always have the luxury of working in such environments, but the habit of productive reflection can be useful even in less forgiving corporate cultures.

If you hang on long enough, people will start calling you "experienced," but that should not be your goal. All experience indicates is that you have been able to survive. It does not indicate the amount you have learned, only the time you have spent. In certain parts of our industry, it is quite easy to repeat the same year of experience 10 times without making significant progress in your abilities. In fact, this sometimes can turn into anti-experience: the phenomenon where every additional year or experience merely reinforces the bad habits you have picked up.[‡] This is why your goal should be to become skilled rather than experienced. The increase in your skill level is the only meaningful testament to the effort you have spent inspecting, adapting, and improving your working habits.

Action

Draw a Personal Practices Map for your working habits. Concentrate on the connections between any practices that have not changed in a while. Ask yourself how your map would change if you discovered that one of those practices was actually counterproductive. Closely examine one of those practices and find out if there are other ways to achieve the same goal. These don't have to be better ways; it's enough for them to be different. Now ask yourself what would happen to your map if you were to adopt one of these different practices.

[†] The Retrospective Prime Directive: *http://www.retrospectives.com/pages/retroPrimeDirective.html*.

[‡] Anti-Experience: *http://c2.com/cgi/wiki/changes.cgi?AntiExperience*.

Record What You Learn

**You should not also underestimate the power of writing
itself....You can lose your larger sense of purpose. But
writing lets you step back and think through a problem.
Even the angriest rant forces the writer to achieve a degree
of thoughtfulness.**

—*Atul Gawande, Better*

Context

You learn the same lessons again and again. They never seem to stick. You often find yourself repeatedly doing things such as setting up CruiseControl, modeling hierarchies in SQL, or introducing patterns to a team. You remember doing very similar things in the past, but the exact details escape you.

Problem

Those who do not learn from history are doomed to repeat it.

Solution

Keep a record of your journey in a journal, personal wiki, or blog. A chronological record of the lessons you have learned can provide inspiration to those you mentor, since it makes your journey explicit, but it can also give you a vital resource to draw upon. Those who use this pattern sooner or later experience a moment when they're searching for the answer to a tricky problem and their search engine gives them a link to their own wiki or blog.

Using a blog to record the lessons you've learned also has the side benefit of helping you meet Kindred Spirits, while a wiki that has accidental linking allows you to see the connections between your experiences.

Try to avoid falling into the trap of just writing down your lessons and forgetting them. Your notebook, blog, or wiki should be a nursery, not a graveyard—lessons should be born from this record, rather than going there to die. You make this happen by regularly going back to read what you've written. Try to make new connections every time you review the material. This process of creative review can lead you to reevaluate old decisions based on new data, or it can reinforce beliefs that were wavering. Either outcome is fine, as long as you don't stagnate. By reviewing your journal, you can switch your past and your present around in order to generate your future.

Ade uses two instances of the same wiki, one for his private thoughts and the other for stuff he wants to share with the world. Keeping a private record as well as a public record means that you get the best of both worlds. Your public record becomes a means of sharing the lessons you have learned and gaining feedback from a wider community; the private record allows you to be painfully honest with yourself about the progress you are making. Having both internal and external feedback loops can give you increased confidence that you are maintaining an accurate self-assessment.

When Dave was Reading Constantly during his apprenticeship, he kept a text file in which he transcribed all the quotes that shaped his learning. Over the years, that file grew to contain over 500 quotes, and Dave eventually decided to upload it and share it online.§ This proved to be an excellent source of references when Dave started writing articles and this book.

Also keep in mind that your choice of record-keeping tool can also be an important Breakable Toy.

This pattern is similar to Share What You Learn, but there the emphasis is on preparing to become a journeyman by improving your ability to communicate with honesty and humility. Here the emphasis is on preserving the route you took to mastery so that in future you can extract new lessons from it.

Action

Grab a paper notebook and start jotting down your thoughts about this book and any ideas it inspires. Make sure your notes have a date on them. Once you've finished this book, keep using the same notebook in the same way for the other things you learn. Over time these entries may become the basis for blog posts, magazine articles, or even a book.

See Also

"Breakable Toys" (page 79), "Kindred Spirits" (page 64), "Read Constantly" (page 102), and "Share What You Learn" (page 89).

Share What You Learn

I can not overstate how much a generous spirit contributes to good luck. Look at the luckiest people around you, the ones you envy, the ones who seem to have destiny falling habitually into their laps. What are they doing that singles them out? It isn't dumb luck if it happens repeatedly. If they're anything like the fortunate people I know, they're prepared, they're always working

§ *http://redsquirrel.com/dave/quotes.html*

> **at their craft, they're alert, they involve their friends in**
> **their work, and they tend to make others feel lucky to be**
> **around them.**
>
> *—Twyla Tharp, The Creative Habit*

Context

You have been an apprentice for a little while. You know a few things and people are starting to look to you as a source of knowledge.

Problem

Up until now, you have focused exclusively on your own improvement as a craftsman. To become a journeyman you will need the ability to communicate effectively and bring other people up to speed quickly.

Solution

Early in your apprenticeship, develop the habit of regularly sharing the lessons you have learned. This may take the form of maintaining a blog or running "brown bag" sessions amongst your Kindred Spirits. You can also make presentations at conferences or write tutorials for the various technologies and techniques that you are learning.

At first this will be difficult. After all, you are not a master or even a journeyman: surely you should wait for someone more experienced to put themselves forward? However, you will find that your fellow apprentices will appreciate one of their own trying to demystify complex topics. You may know only a tiny amount about category theory or prototype-based programming languages, but the little knowledge you have is still more than most. Since you know only a little bit, your explanations will be simple and straight to the point without assuming prior knowledge. This will make them better explanations. You may find that it helps to write the tutorial you wish you had been given when you were first learning a particular topic or technology.

Being part of a community of individuals where both learning on your own and humbly sharing that newly acquired knowledge are valued is one of the most powerful aspects of apprenticeship. It makes otherwise-esoteric fields of knowledge suddenly accessible, and provides apprentices with guides who speak their language.

Furthermore, teaching is a powerful learning tool for the person doing the teaching, perhaps even more so than for the students. Thus the old saying "When one person teaches, two people learn."

This pattern is most clearly connected to Record What You Learn. If you have recorded the things you have learned, it is easier to share them with others. On the other hand, this pattern carries the risk that people won't always appreciate the things you share.

Some lessons should not be shared, and it's important to keep in mind that there is an ethical dimension to knowledge. Before sharing something, consider whether that lesson is yours to share. It may be a secret, or it may harm others. Things that seem obvious to you because of your current context may in fact be your employer's "secret sauce" and it is all too easy as an apprentice to overlook the consequences (legal, financial, and political) of sharing that knowledge.

Other lessons cannot be shared without damaging your relationships with the members of your current team or with your employer. The gains made through the application of Sweep the Floor can easily be undone if others, rightly or wrongly, feel that you are insufficiently humble in the way you share or that you are sharing your lessons due to some ulterior motive.

Be the Worst steers you toward better learning opportunities at the risk of neglecting your responsibilities to the craft. You could fall into a perpetual mode of selfishly sponging knowledge by constantly looking for opportunities to accelerate your learning without ever considering the people who would benefit were you to Share What You Learn.

Dave Smith's pattern Prepare the Way has strong connections to Share What You Learn:

> Prepare The Way raises the bar, teaching that as groundbreakers, we have the additional responsibility of leaving a well-marked, safe trail in our wake as we trundle off into the wilderness.
>
> —*http://c2.com/cgi/wiki?PrepareTheWay*

Action

Think back to the last significant lesson you learned. Write a blog post about it. Provide the information you wish had existed and that would have helped you learn.

Having written the blog post, imagine you're being asked to prepare a workshop for a conference that will teach other people the same lesson. Sketch out that workshop. See if the act of thinking about how you would teach others in an engaging way causes you to rethink the lesson and the blog post.

See Also

"Be the Worst" (page 58), "Kindred Spirits" (page 64), "Record What You Learn" (page 88), and "Sweep the Floor" (page 68).

Create Feedback Loops

We in the software industry are working with a more or less invisible product, yet this very invisibility only heightens our need for feedback.

—Jerry Weinberg in Norm Kerth's Project Retropsectives

Context

You can't tell if you're suffering from "unconscious incompetence" since, as Justin Kruger and David Dunning put it in their article of the same name, those who are unskilled are often unaware of it. Moreover, the less skilled you are, the worse you are at assessing the skills of yourself and others. Success or failure tends to come as a surprise, and what little feedback you receive is an abrupt shock to your self-assessment instead of a support mechanism to help you improve.

Problem

Your self-assessment is only relative to the abilities you used to have, and will always lack objectivity. The teams you work with can easily skew your sense of your own competence. Being on an above-average team can either make you feel like a superstar when you're really more of a backup singer, or destroy your self-confidence when everybody seems so much more competent than you. On the other hand, a below-average team can make you feel complacently smug. Even if you use Reflect as You Work, it will only help you analyze the past rather than inform you about the present.

Solution

Create mechanisms for regularly gathering more or less objective external data about your performance. By soliciting feedback early, often, and effectively, you increase the probability that you will at least be conscious of your incompetence.

There are a variety of mechanisms available for acquiring feedback. At one level these include using techniques like test-driven development or dynamically type-checked languages with interactive interpreters to cause your programs to fail fast. At another level you may acquire feedback by getting your code reviewed or by pair programming. Exams and certifications can also be useful metrics for gauging your ability compared to others, although these often test only your exam-taking technique rather than your skill. Another way of gaining feedback is to ask people how they think you are doing; for example, contact people who interview you for a new job or promotion and ask them their opinion of you. Even if you didn't get the job, you can gain a lot from being told precisely why you were turned down. Sometimes this feedback will reveal facets (both positive and negative) of your personality that you were unaware of.

All of the mechanisms described above will be useless if you haven't developed the ability to process the raw data. For instance, if your employer provides annual reviews, you have to be able to separate the wheat from the chaff in order to get to the useful feedback. Criticism on its own is seldom useful feedback because it doesn't tell you what is expected of you. Other kinds of bad feedback include feedback that is more about the other person than you (e.g., "Do this because I did it when I was your age"), that is really disguised advice, or that is what Dave Winer calls "stop energy."|| This usually manifests itself as well-meaning advice telling you why you can't achieve your goals and should give up immediately rather than risking failure.

So what does useful feedback look like? Useful feedback is data that can be acted upon and that gives you the option of doing more or less of a certain behavior. If you can't do anything about it, then it's not useful feedback. Or at least it's not useful today. If your circumstances change it may suddenly become highly relevant. Try to keep in mind the advice that "if you count something interesting, you will learn something interesting" (*Better*, p. 255).

It's also important to be aware of the distinction that systems thinkers make between reinforcing and balancing feedback. Reinforcing feedback encourages you to do more of something. Balancing feedback encourages you to do less of something. By combining the two types of feedback, a system can be kept relatively stable by making lots of small adjustments. Successful apprentices learn to create situations where they can quickly and frequently receive data about whether they need to do more or less of an activity. This often means learning to communicate your ideas and listening without interrupting.

Acquiring the ability to avoid defending your current level of knowledge in favor of paying careful attention to any feedback is one of the ways in which this pattern overlaps with The White Belt. Both patterns emphasize the idea that the apprentice should strive to become more teachable so that the pool of potential teachers expands.

Patrick finds out what happens if you don't get feedback

When I finally got to coding on the main project, I didn't really have a good understanding of the Oracle framework and how things were supposed to work. I ended up using code written by a senior in another team as the basis for the patterns in which my code was written, as my immediate seniors would rarely give me any feedback. I had no idea if what I was doing was correct even though I was constantly asking. After a while, I discovered that the way I was implementing things was not the preferred way of developing apps and so I asked the engineer whom I copied why it was so. I was lucky that we were still in the "research" phase of our development process so the code I wrote could be fixed.

|| "What is Stop Energy?" Available at: *http://radio.weblogs.com/0107584/stories/2002/05/05/ stopEnergyByDaveWiner.html*.

The hardest thing I found was that there are not many people out there that like to tell you you're making mistakes, so half the battle is trying to find someone who will tell you as soon as possible. Upon reflection, I think an apprentice probably shouldn't work on not making mistakes early as much as they should be working out how to identify the mistakes you make. Once the apprentice identifies their mistakes, it becomes much easier to then learn from them.

—Patrick Kua, email

Action

Find something in your working environment that you can measure and, more importantly, affect. Track that metric for a while. As it changes, ask yourself what it's telling you about your world. See if you can use it (and other metrics) to understand the effects of the changes you are making to your working environment.

See Also

"Reflect As You Work" (page 85) and "The White Belt" (page 18).

Learn How You Fail

Ingenuity is often misunderstood. It is not a matter of superior intelligence but of character. It demands more than anything a willingness to recognize failure, to not paper over the cracks, and to change. It arises from deliberate, even obsessive, reflection on failure and a constant searching for new solutions.

—Atul Gawande, Better

Context

Failure is inevitable. It happens to everybody sooner or later. In fact, someone who has never failed at anything has either avoided pushing at the boundaries of their abilities or has learned to overlook their own mistakes.

Problem

Your learning skills have enhanced your successes, but your failures and weaknesses remain.

Solution

Seek to identify the ways in which you tend to fail and try to resolve those that are worth fixing.

This is not about wallowing in self-pity about past mistakes nor is it an exercise in seeking perfection. Instead, the goal is to gain self-knowledge about the patterns, conditions, habits, and behaviors that lead you to failure. Armed with that self-knowledge, you can make conscious choices and temper the tendency toward idealism when applying "Draw Your Own Map" (page 47) with an awareness of your boundaries and limitations.

By becoming conscious of the things that trip you up, you allow yourself the choice between working to fix these problems or cutting your losses. Accept that there will be some things that you're not good at, or that would require a disproportionate investment of time and effort in order to make a small improvement.

This feeds into your accurate self-assessment, but it also enables you to set realistic limitations on your goals. You can't excel at everything, and accepting these limitations is important, as it forces you to consciously acknowledge distractions and focus on your goals. It may mean accepting that you're never going to make the time for that part-time PhD course, or it may mean letting go of old areas of expertise because you can't devote the time to maintain those skills.

For example, Ade keeps a set of pages on his private wiki listing his current skillset and his limitations or boundaries. This enables him to select which boundaries to push outward (e.g., try maintaining a large codebase in a dynamically type-checked language) and where to stop wasting effort (e.g., accept that the 6502 assembler for the Commodore 64 is unlikely to undergo a massive resurgence).

Action

In the programming language of your choice, use a simple text editor (later on you will see why it's important that you don't use an IDE for this exercise) to write an implementation of binary search in one sitting. Do not compile or run it yet. Now, write all the tests that you think you will need to verify that you have a correct implementation. Keep note of the bugs and problems you discover at this stage. Now, still without compiling or running the tests, go back and fix all the problems that you have discovered so far. Iterate until you're satisfied that the code and the tests are both perfect. Finally, try to compile and run the tests. Most people will discover corner cases they hadn't thought of and trivial little errors. Before you fix these errors, try to understand how they could have occurred in something you were sure was perfect. What does that tell you about yourself? Write down what you learn in the iterations between what you thought was perfect code and the point when you have code that actually compiles and passes all the tests. If you're feeling particularly brave, get a friend to review the code and see what else she can discover.

See Also

"Draw Your Own Map" (page 47).

Wrapping Up

Perpetual Learning can be viewed as a blessing or a curse. Learning something new can be painful, especially when it is done under pressure and with little guidance. Yet, like the athlete who must endure muscle soreness after strenuous workouts, the software developer endures the mental dissonance that comes with learning something new. That dissonance can become a welcome sign of progress. Self-reflection, identifying failure through feedback loops, and learning your weaknesses all appear negative on the surface, but these patterns are helping you to reduce your ignorance. The alternative is to focus exclusively on what you *already* know, but this is not the way toward mastering software craftsmanship; it is the way to specialization in a single expertise. Phillip Armour, in his paper "The Five Orders of Ignorance," focuses on the roles of ignorance and knowledge in software development:

> Software is not a product, it's a medium for storing knowledge. Therefore, software development is not a product producing activity, it is a knowledge acquiring activity. Knowledge is just the other side of the coin of ignorance, therefore software development is an ignorance-reduction activity.

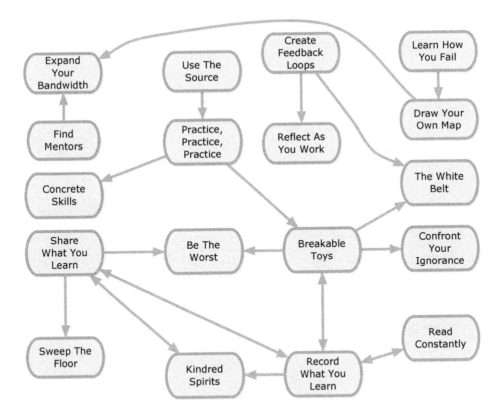

CHAPTER SIX

Construct Your Curriculum

He'd no longer be a grade-motivated person. He'd be a knowledge-motivated person. He would need
no external pushing to learn. His push would come from the inside.... Motivation of this sort, once it
catches hold, is a ferocious force.

—Robert Pirsig, *Zen and the Art of Motorcycle Maintenance*

We live in an age of abundant information. The invention of the printing press ushered in an era that allows even some of the poorest members of society to acquire the knowledge, and therefore the power, to change their circumstances. The ever-expanding World Wide Web and an unending series of technical innovations continue to lower the barriers to virtually any information we could ever want. As our Internet bandwidth increases and our handheld devices store a seemingly limitless amount of data, we can now access high-resolution media in text, audio, and video formats anywhere, at any time. Like any good apprentice, you will likely use the latest and greatest devices and media platforms, but there is certain information that is mainly found in plain old low-tech books. While blogs can provide an excellent stream of reading material, the vast amounts of wisdom captured in the books of experienced practitioners like Jerry Weinberg, Fred Brooks, Steve McConnell, and Kent Beck cannot be replaced, not even with higher-bandwidth information. Even if you're not a bookworm, a successful apprenticeship needs to include some books as well as time devoted to studying. You're not in school, though. There is no assigned reading—it's up to you to find recommendations and construct your own curriculum.

Reading List

> No one can learn everything at once, but no principle or rule prevents the apprentice from learning a little of this today, a little of that tomorrow, things in some order no one ever thought of before, or learning to the point where he wants to stop and then switching to something else. He need not, when he wants to learn a certain procedure, wait until it's time in a prearranged schedule; nor need he learn something he is not ready for, thinks uninteresting, frightening, or unnecessary. The learner makes his own curriculum.

—Howard S. Becker, *"A School Is a Lousy Place to Learn Anything In"*

Context

After developing enough competence and skill to become proficient in Your First Language, you're beginning to look around and see the incredible amount of information you still need to learn.

Problem

The number of books you need to read is increasing faster than you can read them.

Solution

Maintain a Reading List to track the books you plan to read, and remember the books you've read.

In the spirit of the Share What You Learn pattern, consider storing your list in a public space. This will allow other people to benefit from the things you learn. We use the wiki at *http:// bookshelved.org* (started by Laurent Bossavit in 2002), but any public list would work just as well. Ideally, your list would allow you to sequence the books, while distinguishing which books you've read and when.

This pattern is not just about managing the books you plan to read. It is also a mechanism for reflecting on your past reading habits. With data spanning several years, you can start to see patterns, trends, and gaps in the things you're choosing to study. This can help you make better decisions about what to read next. If you make this information publicly available, then there is the possibility that other people will contribute suggestions for future reading. This can help you discover hidden connections and obscure gems.

One of the most valuable things you can gain from any book is a list of other books that are worth reading. Over time, you will discover that certain books keep popping up in bibliographies, and you should move those books to the top of your reading list. Other books will drop down. Since your reading list is actually a priority queue, you will eventually realize that certain books have fallen so far in the ranking that you will probably never read them. This is fine. The purpose of this pattern is to give you a way to prioritize and filter the flood of potential knowledge.

The main difficulty with implementing this pattern is that you need a deep understanding of a topic in order to work out which books to read and in which order. One way to resolve this paradox is to initially pick books that give you a broad understanding of the topic in question, and then select books that drill down into the specific aspects that interest you. The other way to resolve this paradox is to depend on your Kindred Spirits and your mentors. Your mentors will be able to recommend must-read books, while discussion with your fellow apprentices can help you work out the order in which to read them. You can also take advantage of the public reading lists provided by other people who are implementing this pattern.

Another difficulty lies figuring out where to start. You can find an excellent list of books to populate your Reading List in Chapter 35 of *Code Complete*, Microsoft Press, and in the bibliography of *The Pragmatic Programmer*. You can also take a look at the bibliography for this book to see some of the books that inspired us.

This pattern owes a debt to Ravi Mohan's idea of a Book Chain[*] and to the Sequential Study pattern from Joshua Kerievsky's pattern language for study groups.[†] Whereas Book Chain is

---

[*] *http://ravimohan.blogspot.com/2005/08/apprenticeship-pattern.html*

[†] *http://www.industriallogic.com/papers/khdraft.pdf*

about asking people to recommend sets of books that will introduce you to a new topic, this pattern is more about managing the continuous stream of books you find interesting. This pattern also differs from Sequential Study because it doesn't focus on reading books in chronological order to understand the way they influence each other. In this pattern, the book you should read next is the one that takes you can step further on your journey.

It is important to remember that this is *your* Reading List. It's great to be influenced by the suggestions of others, but only you truly know your current context. Therefore, you should be the one making the choice about what to study next. That said, it's also important to read the right book at the right time. Doing so is far more powerful than churning through a bunch of books you don't have the experience or depth of knowledge to truly understand. Too many people read *Design Patterns* too early in their studies, when a book like *Refactoring* would be a much gentler introduction to patterns. Find Mentors and ask them for advice about which book you should read next. Timing has a powerful impact on your experience with a book.

Action

Create a text file, perhaps putting it under source control. Type in all the books you're currently reading. This is your Reading List, and the simplest possible implementation of this pattern. Now all you have to do is keep this text file up to date.

See Also

"Find Mentors" (page 61), "Kindred Spirits" (page 64), "Share What You Learn" (page 89), and "Your First Language" (page 13).

Read Constantly

If you read even one good programming book every two months, roughly 35 pages a week, you'll soon have a firm grasp on the industry and distinguish yourself from nearly everyone around you.

—*Steve McConnell, Code Complete*

Context

You have Unleashed Your Enthusiasm to open lots and lots of doors.

Problem

There seems to be an endless stream of deeper and more fundamental concepts that are eluding you, despite your proficiency at Your First Language.

Solution

Focus your thirst for learning on consuming as much of the written word as possible. Emphasize books over blogs as you construct your Reading List.

There should be seasons of The Long Road when you have (or take) the opportunity to read a significant number of books. For Dave, this was in 2002–2003, a couple years after he started programming and just as he was hitting a plateau in his first language, Perl. This season was enabled by public transportation: Dave had about 90 minutes a day on the train to read whatever he wanted. He was so intent that he would continue reading when he got off the train and walked the mile to his cubicle. Immersing yourself in the classics and primary sources of the field provides an unparalleled education when coupled with Finding Mentors and frequent interactions with Kindred Spirits.

Part of this immersion should include exploring the vast warehouse of knowledge that is the academic community. Reading the occasional research paper will stretch your mind and keep you in touch with the cutting edge of computer science, and also offers a source of challenging new ideas. Trying to implement these ideas will expand your toolbox with new algorithms, data structures, and design patterns many years before they reach the mainstream.

Action

By reading this book, you have already begun to apply this pattern. The trick is to keep up the momentum after you've finished this book. Decide now what your next book will be. Buy or borrow it so that when you finish this book, you can switch immediately to the next one.

You should also try to keep a slim book with you at all times. This will let you use the little bits of dead time throughout each day (such as train journeys or waiting in queues) to learn.

See Also

"Find Mentors" (page 61), "Kindred Spirits" (page 64), "Reading List" (page 100), "The Long Road" (page 38), "Unleash Your Enthusiasm" (page 22), and "Your First Language" (page 13).

Study the Classics

Discover the great literature in your profession or area of interest—the finest books, articles, and speeches ever written—and then begin an earnest study of these works.

—*Joshua Kerievsky in "Knowledge Hydrant: A Pattern Language for Study Groups"‡*

Context

You are self-taught, or had a highly practical education that valued skills training over theory.

Problem

The experienced people you collaborate with are constantly referencing concepts such as Brooks' law from books that they assume you—and any self-respecting software developer—have read.

Solution

Expose Your Ignorance and ask about the unknown concept and the book it came from. Add this book to your Reading List.

Joshua Kerievsky once asked Jerry Weinberg how he keeps up with all the books that come out. Jerry said, "Easy—I only read the great ones" (*Refactoring to Patterns*, p. 33). By Reading Constantly and Reflecting as You Work, you will, like Jerry, eventually be able to "only read the good ones." When you pick up a book and the first thing you wonder is how out of date it is, you're reading the wrong kind of books. Successful apprentices tend to focus on "long-lived books" and use the Web or experimentation to learn how the information has evolved. Dave remembers vividly the experience of reading his first classic in this field, The Psychology of Computer Programming, and marveling at how relevant the book felt, despite the stories of punch cards and room-sized computers. The wisdom captured in such classics is vital information to keep you heading in the right direction on The Long Road.

One danger of focusing on the classics is taking it too far and abandoning the more pragmatic knowledge and information that enables you to improve your day-to-day craftsmanship. Be sure to intermingle classics with modern, pragmatic books and/or articles in your Reading List.

‡ *http://www.industriallogic.com/papers/khdraft.pdf*

Action

What is the oldest book in your pile? Read that one first. The next time you're flicking through another developer's book collection, take note of the oldest books and ask the developer why she still owns them.

See Also

"Expose Your Ignorance" (page 25), "Read Constantly" (page 102), "Reading List" (page 100), "Reflect As You Work" (page 85), and "The Long Road" (page 38).

Dig Deeper

In practice, algorithm problems do not arise at the beginning of a large project. Rather, they typically arise as subproblems when it suddenly becomes clear that the programmer does not know how to proceed or that the current program is inadequate.

—Steven S. Skiena, The Algorithm Design Manual

Context

You live in a world of tight deadlines and complex software projects that use a multitude of tools. Your employers cannot afford the luxury of employing enough specialists to fill every role. You learn only enough about any tool to get today's job done. You select a handful of tutorials on the language or library that you're working with today. You make decisions without taking the time to understand the issues, and copy the toy examples provided with the tools. This works to the extent that you can turn your hand to anything. You acquire the ability to dive into a new technology and come up with a solution very quickly. You only ever learn the parts of a technology that you need to get your portion of the system working, and you depend on other members of the team to learn the other parts. For instance, you may be a server-side Java developer, and consequently have little or no knowledge of how the user interface was built.

Problem

You keep running into difficulty maintaining the code you've written because it turns out that the tutorials you followed cut corners and simplified complex issues. You find that your superficial knowledge of a thousand tools means you're always floundering whenever a subtle bug arises or you have to do something that demands deep knowledge. People often accuse you of having a misleading CV because you don't distinguish between a couple of weeks of extending an existing web service and a deep knowledge of the issues inherent in maintaining an interoperable and highly scalable enterprise system. What's even worse is that because your knowledge is so superficial, you're not even aware of how little you know until something or someone puts you to the test.

Solution

Learn to dig deep into tools, technologies, and techniques. Acquire the depths of knowledge to the point that you know why things are the way they are. Depth means understanding the forces that led to a design rather than just the details of a design. For instance, it means understanding type theory (or at least the simplification offered by the typing quadrant at *http://c2.com/cgi/wiki?TypingQuadrant*) rather than simply parroting the things you've heard others say.

As one of our ex-colleagues (Ravi Mohan, personal communication) found:

> A knowledge of the various forms of concurrency (and their limits) is more useful knowledge than "subclass Thread or implement Runnable."

The areas where you have deep knowledge feed your confidence and guide you when you are deciding how to apply Sweep the Floor, because they indicate places where you can deliver value early in your time with a new team. More importantly, this depth of knowledge is something you can fall back on to give you the strength to tackle new areas. You can always say to yourself: "If I mastered EJBs then I can handle metaclasses."

Another advantage of digging deep into a technology is that you can actually explain what's going on beneath the surface of the systems you work on. In interviews, this understanding will distinguish you from other candidates who can't describe the software they've helped build in a meaningful way because all they understand is one little portion. Once you're part of a team, it's the application of this pattern that separates out those who are making random piles of rubble (the Pragmatic Programmers called this "programming by coincidence" while Steve McConnell calls it "cargo cult software engineering") from those who are building cathedrals.

How do we spot the cathedral builders? They are the ones on your team who end up doing the debugging, decompiling, and reverse-engineering, and who read the specification, RFC, or standards for the technologies you use. The people who do this have made a shift in perspective and built up a practiced understanding of the tools that support them.

This shift in perspective involves wanting to follow a problem down through the layers of a system and being willing to spend the time to acquire the knowledge that will make sense of it all. For instance, switching from a single core to a multicore laptop might alter the behavior of your Java concurrency tests. Some people will just shrug and accept that their tests will now behave unpredictably. Others will trace the problem down to the CPU level via the concurrency libraries, the Java Memory Model, and the specification of the physical hardware.

The tools you need to be familiar with include debuggers (like GDB, PDB, and RDB), which let you see into your running program; wire-level debuggers (like Wireshark), which let you see network traffic; and the willingness to read specifications. Being able to read specifications as well as code means that nothing is hidden from you. It gives you the ability to ask hard questions about the libraries you use, and if you don't like the answers you get, you are capable of reimplementing them yourself or moving to a more standards-compliant implementation.

One of the ways to use this pattern is to get your information from primary sources. This means that the next time someone talks to you about Representation State Transfer, better known as REST, you should take that as an excuse to read Roy Fielding's PhD thesis in which he defined the concept. Consider writing a blog post to clarify or share what you've learned, and to encourage others to read the original document as well.

Don't just take the word of someone who is quoting a book that paraphrased an article that mentioned the Wikipedia page that links to the original IETF Request for Comment document. To truly understand any idea, you need to reconstruct the context in which it was first expressed. This lets you verify that the essence of the idea survived going through all those middlemen.

Find out who first came up with the ideas and understand the problems they were trying to solve. This kind of context usually gets lost in translation as the idea gets passed around. Sometimes you will find that seemingly new ideas were abandoned long ago, often for good reasons—but everybody has long since forgotten about it because the original context has been lost. Many times you will find that the original source of an idea is a much better teacher than the chain of people who have been selectively quoting each other for years. Whatever happens, tracing the lineage of ideas you have found helpful is an important exercise, and a habit that will serve you well through the years as you attempt to learn new things.

When you read a tutorial, you should not be looking for code to copy but for a mental structure in which to place your new knowledge. Your goal should be to understand the historical context of the concept and whether it is a special instance of something else. Ask yourself if there appears to be some underlying computer science concept behind what you are learning, and what trade-offs were made in the implementation that you are using. Armed with this deeper knowledge, you should be able to go beyond the initial tutorial when you run into problems.

For example, people often run into trouble with regular expressions because they only acquire a superficial understanding. You can get along just fine for years, maybe even decades, without really understanding the difference between a Deterministic Finite Automaton and a Nondeterministic Finite Automaton. Then one day your wiki stops working. It turns out that if your regular expression engine is implemented recursively, then on certain inputs that require backtracking it will run for a very long time and eventually throw a StackOverflowException. Ade discovered this the hard way, but luckily it happened on his toy wiki implementation and not in a production environment.

With all this focus on understanding technologies and tools in depth, you need to take care not to accidentally become a narrow specialist. The goal is to be able to acquire as much specialized knowledge as necessary to solve any problem, without losing your perspective about the relative importance of different aspects of software development.

One thing you will learn from trying to apply this pattern is that gaining deep knowledge is hard. This is why most people's knowledge of the computer science that supports software development is a mile wide and an inch thick. It is easier and often more profitable to depend on other people's knowledge of the fundamentals than to spend the extra effort to acquire it yourself. You can tell yourself that you can always learn it when you need it; however, when that day comes you'll need to know everything by the end of the week, but it will take a month just to learn all the prerequisites.

Another possible consequence of possessing only surface knowledge is that you may never realize that the problem you are trying to solve either has a well-known solution or is in fact impossible (in this case, there may be a lot of academic papers on why it's impossible and how to redefine the problem to make it soluble). If you're only skimming the surface, then you won't know the things you don't know, and without understanding the bounds of your knowledge you can't discover new things. Often the process of burrowing through all the layers of a problem will reveal an underlying concept from computer science. While the work of computer scientists can seem impractical, those who can apply the most advanced theories to real-world problems gain the ability to do things that can seem almost magical to others. Simple changes in your choice of algorithm or data structure can turn a batch job that takes months to run into something that finishes before the user has even let go of the mouse button. Someone who only knows about Lists, Sets, and HashMaps is unlikely to realize that he needs a Trie to solve his problem. Instead, he will just assume that a problem like longest-prefix matching is impossibly hard, and will either give up or ask if the feature can be deprioritized.

If you apply this pattern regularly, you will become one of those people who truly understand how their tools work. You will no longer just be gluing bits of code together and depending on other people's magic to do the heavy lifting. Be aware that this understanding will separate you from the vast majority of programmers you work with, and will make you the logical choice for the most difficult assignments. Consequently, you will be the most likely to fail completely or succeed spectacularly. In addition, do not allow this knowledge to make you arrogant. Instead, continue to seek out opportunities to Be the Worst. Challenge yourself to assemble useful tools from these fundamental building blocks, rather than just basking in your ability to take things apart.

Action

Find and read RFC 2616, which describes HTTP1.1, and RFC 707, which describes the state of the art in Remote Procedure Call technology as of January 1976. Armed with your deeper knowledge of HTTP, try to implement a client and a server for RFC 707. When you feel you have a good understanding of the trade-offs made by the editors of RFC 707, examine a modern open source implementation of the same ideas, such as the Apache Thrift framework that powers Facebook. Then, from your informed vantage point, write a blog post describing the evolution of our knowledge regarding remote procedure calls and distributed systems over the last three decades.

Now, go and read Steve Vinoski's articles about RPC. Do you now have doubts about the depth of your understanding? Write a blog post about your doubts and your current level of understanding.

See Also

"Be the Worst" (page 58) and "Sweep the Floor" (page 68).

Familiar Tools

> **A rut is when you're spinning your wheels and staying in place; the only progress you make is in digging yourself a deeper rut. A groove is different: The wheels turn and you move forward effortlessly...a rut is the consequence of sticking to tried and tested methods that don't take into account how you or the world has changed.**
>
> —*Twyla Tharp, The Creative Habit*

Context

Every project is filled with new things to learn. There are new team members, new roles within the team, new business domains, new techniques, and new technology.

Problem

Amid all this flux, something has to stay the same, or you might as well be engaged in research. How can you provide any guarantees about anything to your customer? When you say it will take a certain amount of time to deliver some feature, your customers need some basis for their confidence in your ability to deliver.

Solution

Identify and focus on a set of familiar tools. Ideally, these are the tools where you no longer need the documentation—you either know all the best practices, gotchas, and FAQs by heart, or you have written them down on your blog, wiki, or wherever you have chosen to Record

What You Learn. Armed with this knowledge, you can provide reliable estimates about certain parts of your work, limiting the risk to the new and unexplored areas.

Just because these tools are familiar to you doesn't mean you should always recommend them to others. Sometimes the best tool for the job and the one you're most familiar with are different. At those times, you have to decide if your productivity is more important than the team's productivity. Just because you know Struts like the back of your hand doesn't necessarily make it easy to use.

Still, these are the tools you carry with you from project to project. They're part of what makes you more productive than the next candidate being interviewed. If you run into problems, you already know where to go for answers. You know the problems these tools solve and the problems they cause. Consequently, you know where *not* to use them, which is as important as knowing where they are best applied.

Over time, you will grow more and more comfortable with this small set of tools. This has benefits, in the form of increased productivity, but it also holds dangers. If you are not careful, you may start to view your familiar tools as "golden hammers," capable of solving any problem. There is also the danger that you may become such an expert in these tools that you are unable to let go of them, or even to recognize when better tools emerge.

The real challenge comes when you need to throw away a large part of your toolbox. Sometimes your tools will become obsolete; other times you will discover that there are better tools out there. In rare cases, your familiarity with the "state of the art" will lead you to invent something that invalidates the tools you already know.

> In a time of drastic change it is the learners who inherit the future. The learned usually find themselves equipped to live in a world that no longer exists.
>
> —Eric Hoffer, *Reflections on the Human Condition*

Ade was a very early adopter of the centralized source control system called Subversion. As it became more popular, clients would seek out Ade for their projects because of his Subversion expertise. Despite this, Ade has been tracking the emergence of a new breed of *distributed* source control systems from the beginning.§ By the time Subversion becomes obsolete, its place in Ade's toolbox will already be occupied by Git or Mercurial. Letting go of familiar and valuable tools is a painful process, but it's a skill that you need to acquire.

We can guarantee that the tools you use as an apprentice will be obsolete by the time you become a journeyman. *In time, all of your favorite tools will become junk.* For your career to prosper, you must learn to acquire and abandon familiar tools with ease. Constructing a curriculum that supports this goal is one of the challenges that all apprentices face in the transition to becoming a journeyman.

---

§ Ade's research on potential replacements for Subversion: *http://delicious.com/ade/source-control-renaissance ?setcount=100.*

Action

Write down a list of your familiar tools. If the list has less than five items, start hunting around for tools that will fill the gaps in your toolbox. This may simply be a matter of identifying a tool you already use but don't know well enough, or it may involve finding new tools altogether. Either way, put together a plan for learning these tools and start implementing it today.

If you already have five familiar tools, carefully examine them. Are better and more powerful tools available? Are you clinging to tools that are already obsolete? Are there emerging tools that threaten to render elements of your toolbox obsolete? If the answer to any of these questions is yes, then start the process of replacing these tools today. If you need somewhere safe to experiment with new tools, make use of Breakable Toys.

See Also

"Breakable Toys" (page 79).

Wrapping Up

In your formal education, you may have gotten used to having a curriculum presented to you and churning through it with little to no thought about whether these were the best books to be reading, and in the best order. You now need to become an active participant in your ongoing self-education, so that you will grow to be a developer who can wield powerful tools to organize and collect information. You may not know everything you need to know to construct your curriculum, but you have the power to synthesize the wisdom of the many people who will offer you suggestions. Learning to enjoy the learning process itself will serve you well in the ever-changing technology landscape that keeps us perpetually on our toes.

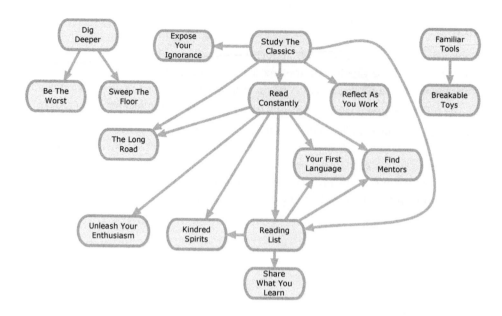

CHAPTER SEVEN

Conclusion

Craftsmen take pride most in skills that mature. This is
why simple imitation is not a sustaining satisfaction; the
skill has to evolve.

—*Richard Sennett, The Craftsman*

When we started writing this book, we merely wanted to provide advice to aspiring
apprentices—those who aspire to a craft. However, there are limitations as well as
opportunities in a craft approach.

The violins and cellos that were made in the workshop of Antonio Stradivari in the 17th and
18th centuries are considered the finest ever made. They regularly sell for millions of dollars,
and over the last 300 years there have been many attempts to reproduce them. However, as
written in *The Craftsman* (p. 75): "the secrets of masters like Antonio Stradivari and Guarneri
del Gesù, have indeed died with them. Mountains of cash and endless experiments have failed
to prize out the secrets of these masters. Something in the character of these workshops must
have inhibited knowledge transfer." As Stradivari got older and could no longer be as active
in the daily life of his apprentices, the quality of the instruments made in his workshop
dropped. Since his workshop "revolved around the extraordinary talents of an individual" and
Stradivari could not pass on his genius to his apprentices, his workshop died with him (*The
Craftsman*, p. 76).

Stradivari's apprentices included his two sons, and he had no incentive to hide anything from
them. As far as we know he taught them everything he knew. Or rather, he taught them
everything he thought was important for them to know. He failed precisely because of all the
little bits of tacit knowledge that he wasn't even aware were part of his skillset. His workshop's
downfall was embedded in all the subtle connections that he didn't record because they didn't
seem important at the time, and all the tacit knowledge that he applied whenever he worked
with an apprentice on some seemingly trivial task.

Stradivari didn't share his knowledge widely enough, and neglected to teach his customers how to hold his students to the same standards as himself. Ultimately, the experience he had spent a lifetime gaining died with him. However, we should put this downfall into context. Musicians still describe the work of Stradivari's students as "excellent, but no more than that" (*The Craftsman*, p. 77). The lesson we should learn from the example of the supremely skilled Stradivari is that "masters should be pestered to explain themselves, to dredge out the assemblage of clues and moves they have in silence within" and that we should push them to make the tacit explicit. Without apprentices who are enthusiastic to the point of being pushy, software craftsmanship will continue to exist only in isolated pockets of quality that have formed around small groups of peculiarly talented developers.

Software development is a craft precisely because we don't understand it well enough to make it a codified discipline like science or engineering. Despite the best efforts of groups like the Software Engineering Institute and the Agile Alliance, our field is still one where individual skill is often the most significant determining factor in a project's success. When we use the word *skill*, we don't just mean how much computer science you know or the effectiveness of your development process or how much experience you have. We mean the union of all the things it takes to deliver working software. It includes, but is not limited to, all the lessons you have learned from the patterns in this book.

Skill matters so much because we don't understand what we do well enough to write it down in a format where anyone can apply it and achieve the same results. Our customers would like software projects to be repeatable in the same way as scientific experiments. They would love to be able to hire any team of developers to build their system, safe in the knowledge that as long as the team possesses a minimal level of competence, they'll get what they asked for. Instead, customers have to settle for putting together a team and hoping that it's up to the task. They hope that if a team of a similar size with similar levels of experience was able to build something similar in the past, then maybe today's team can do it too. Unfortunately, the range of skill levels in software development is wide, and the best of us can routinely do things that most of us consider to be impossible.

Moreover, most programmers think they are above average. The sad reality is that, due to the skewed distribution of skill illustrated by the following chart, most programmers are actually *below* average. This may sound counterintuitive, but if you imagine that we, Dave and Ade, are sitting at a table and Bill Gates joins us, then suddenly most of the geeks at that table have a below-average salary. That is to say, the people on the extreme ends of the curve in programming skill skew the distribution. When you combine that with the Dunning-Kruger (or unconscious incompetence) effect, which we discussed in Create Feedback Loops, you begin to see why so many software projects end up as failures. Often there is a mismatch between the skill level we have and the skill level that is needed to solve the problems we face. All we can do is try to improve our methodology. But no process, no matter how agile or lean, can tell you that what you're trying to do is NP-Complete or violates the CAP conjecture. These may seem like obscure concepts to you but there are programmers out there who feel the same about regular expressions or HTTP or Unix. There is no substitute for having this knowledge and these skills if that is what a project needs to succeed.

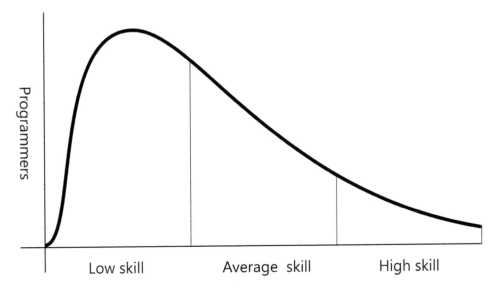

When we say that something is a craft, one of the things we mean is that it is a discipline and a tradition that places a high value on skill. This includes acquiring, growing, and eventually transmitting that skill. We believe true mastery is shown in the effect you have on others by transmitting your superior skill.

In his book entitled *Better: A Surgeon's Notes on Performance Dr. Atul,* Gawande tells the story of the physician Ignac Semmelweis (*Better*, p. 15). In 1847, Semmelweis worked out that "by not washing their hands consistently or well enough, doctors were themselves to blame" for the leading cause of death among women who gave birth in hospitals. He introduced simple practices, like asking doctors to wash their hands with chlorine in between seeing different patients, that reduced the mortality rate from 20% to 1%. However, in the process of achieving his superior results, he managed to alienate or offend his entire profession. Things eventually got so bad that his colleagues started to deliberately avoid washing their hands just to defy him. Semmelweis's failure to properly explain his ideas or convince others eventually cost him his job, and also cost many people their lives in the 20 years it took before Joseph Lister discovered the same ideas. As Gawande puts it, "Semmelweis was a genius but he was also a lunatic, and that made him a failed genius" (*Better*, p. 17).

In the same way, many of the patterns and ideas in this book will generate conflict and resistance. This is partly because there are always people who benefit from the current situation and who fear they may lose something if the situation improves. However, we need to learn from Semmelweis's failure. We can choose to explain our ideas clearly and persuade people to try out our approach. We can also choose to focus on creating a community of organizations that welcome positive change, and seek out people who aspire to mastery.

In software development, we don't know exactly what constitutes mastery, but we do know what it isn't. Being a genius, lucky, rich, or famous doesn't make you a master. These things aren't essential to craftsmanship. Skill across all facets of software development and the ability to transmit that skill in ways that move the discipline forward are at the heart of the craft.

One of the ways in which we can spot masters is that their students eventually surpass them in ambition and in achievement. Masters understand the danger of unquestioning deference to their authority, in that "the pursuit of excellence can create problems for longevity of organizations as in Stradivari's workshop. Here the experience of doing high-quality work was contained in the master's own tacit knowledge, which meant his excellence could not be passed on to the next generation" (*The Craftsman*, p. 243). As an apprentice, you should aim to become better than your teachers. And if they are good teachers, they should try to help you achieve that goal.

Mastery isn't something that a person can claim for herself, as human vanity puts a limit on how accurate our self-assessment can ever be. If someone claims to be a master, ask her for her credentials. Does she point to her work? Assessing the work of someone who is more skilled than you are is notoriously difficult. You won't understand why the things she makes look so easy are so hard. At best, you will be able to tell that this person is more skilled than you. But that isn't enough for mastery. Being ahead of you on the path doesn't make someone a master.

Does she point to her qualifications? After all, there's no certificate for "Master Software Craftsman." All a candidate for mastery can claim is that her peers and those who she believes are already masters think that she is ready to make the step up. This is admittedly a recursive definition. Only those who are already masters can say you're a master, and you can't tell if the people saying you're a master are good enough to confer that honor until you're a master yourself. Unfortunately there is no other way for a new craft to evolve. All crafts begin by stumbling into the world with unsatisfactory definitions and unclear standards. We have to put up with these until we have built up a community and a body of knowledge that can clearly demonstrate the skill of its practitioners.

Until then the best way to detect mastery is to examine the quality of the person's work and that produced by her apprentices. The work and lives of the apprentices highlight the skill rather than the talent or luck of the master. Mere genius is not mastery, but if a person is able to train others to equal or surpass her genius, then it becomes evident that person is a potential master.

The authors of this book are not masters. At best, we are journeymen sharing what we've learned about the road ahead. On a scale of 1 to 10 we'd rate ourselves as 9s, but sometimes we meet people who make us realize that the scale goes all the way up to 100. There are many practitioners that we deeply respect, but the craft of software development is still lacking masters. This is not a problem. Software is a new craft—at best we've been building software for less than 70 years. So we shouldn't expect to already have master software craftsmen.

How can we be so certain that true masters do not exist? We can't. Masters might exist even though we haven't found them. Absence of proof is not evidence of proof.[*] However, we would expect the existence of master software craftsmen to cause ripples through the whole of the software industry. Not just because their products and tools would be superior, but because their students would be as well. There would be a stream of excellent apprentices and journeymen flowing from particular sources. These students would stick out; their capacity to teach, "learn and change—and to do so faster than everyone else" would mean that they would pull away from the rest of us (*Better*, p. 227). As with Gawande's "positive deviants," these master workshops would be considered strange, but their results would be undeniably superior. Merely copying their practices would deliver significant improvements, but apprenticing yourself to these masters would be the only way to keep up as they continued to get better and better.

If we had told you at the start of the book that there are no masters, you might have been discouraged. Now that you have seen the patterns we have gathered in a few short years and how much of our craft can be learned, we hope you will see this fact as an opportunity and maybe even a challenge. We hope that the apprentices inspired by our work will argue: there are no masters...yet.

[*] Absence of Evidence Is Evidence of Absence: *http://www.overcomingbias.com/2007/08/absence-of-evid.html.*

Pattern List

- A Different Road: You have discovered that the direction you want to go is different from the path toward software craftsmanship.
- Be the Worst: Your learning has decelerated as you've quickly surpassed everyone around you.
- Breakable Toys: You work in an environment that does not allow for failure, yet you need a safe place to learn.
- Concrete Skills: You want to work on a great development team, yet you have very little practical experience.
- Confront Your Ignorance: You have discovered wide gaps in your knowledge, and your work requires that you understand these topics.
- Craft over Art: You need to deliver a solution for your customer, and you can choose from a simpler, proven solution or take the opportunity to create something novel and fantastic.
- Create Feedback Loops: You can't tell if you're suffering from "unconscious incompetence."
- Dig Deeper: You have only superficial knowledge of many tools, technologies, and techniques and keep hitting roadblocks as you try to tackle tougher problems.
- Draw Your Own Map: None of the career paths that your employer provides is a fit for you.
- Expand Your Bandwidth: Your understanding of software development is narrow and focused only on the low-level details of what you've worked on in your day job.
- Expose Your Ignorance: You have discovered wide gaps in your knowledge and are afraid that people will think that you don't know what you're doing.

- Familiar Tools: You are finding it difficult to estimate your work because your toolset and technology stack are changing so rapidly.

- Find Mentors: You find that you're spending a lot of time reinventing wheels and hitting roadblocks, but you aren't sure where to turn for guidance.

- Kindred Spirits: You find yourself stranded without mentors and in an atmosphere that seems at odds with your aspirations.

- Learn How You Fail: Your learning skills have enhanced your successes, but your failures and weaknesses remain.

- Nurture Your Passion: You work in an environment that stifles your passion for the craft.

- Practice, Practice, Practice: The performance of your daily programming activities does not give you room to learn by making mistakes.

- Read Constantly: There seems to be an endless stream of deeper and more fundamental concepts that are eluding you despite your quickly acquired proficiency.

- Reading List: The number of books you need to read is increasing faster than you can read them.

- Record What You Learn: You learn the same lessons again and again, but they never seem to stick.

- Reflect as You Work: As the number of years and projects you have under your belt increases, you find yourself awaiting the epiphany that will magically make you "experienced."

- Retreat into Competence: You feel overwhelmed as you are faced with the vast reaches of your ignorance.

- Rubbing Elbows: You have the feeling that there are superior techniques and approaches to the craft that are eluding you.

- Share What You Learn: You are frustrated that the people around you are not learning as quickly as you are.

- Stay in the Trenches: You have been offered a promotion into a role that will pull you away from programming.

- Study the Classics: The experienced people around you are constantly referencing concepts from books that they assume you have read.

- Sustainable Motivations: You find yourself working in the frustrating world of ambiguously specified projects for customers with shifting and conflicting demands.

- Sweep the Floor: You are an inexperienced developer and need to earn your team's trust.

- The Deep End: You're beginning to fear that your career is not resting on a plateau, but is in fact stuck in a rut.

- The Long Road: You aspire to become a master software craftsman, yet your aspiration conflicts with what people expect from you.

- The White Belt: You are struggling to learn, because the experience you have seems to have somehow made it harder to acquire new skills.
- Unleash Your Enthusiasm: You find yourself holding back your excitement and curiosity about software development in order to fit in with your team.
- Use the Source: How do you find out if your work is any good given that those around you may not have the ability to tell good code from bad?
- Use Your Title: When you introduce yourself in a professional setting, you feel you have to apologize or explain away the difference between your skill level and your job description.
- Your First Language: You are familiar with a few languages, but lack fluency in any of them.

A Call for Apprenticeship

Dave Hoover

NOTE
I posted this on my blog[*] on August 22, 2007. This call to action is aimed at the people who have the power to hire apprentices and establish apprenticeship programs. Even if you don't currently possess this power, I hope that you can keep these words in mind as you move beyond your apprenticeship years.

At Agile 2007 last week, I snuck into the last 30 minutes of Uncle Bob's talk about Craftsmanship and Professionalism. When Uncle Bob talks about Craftsmanship he is generally talking about nitty-gritty details of the craft, such as specific practices and tools, but he did have one slide on apprenticeship. He ranted a bit about how most universities do not equip graduates with sufficient skills to allow them to deliver quality software from day one. (Not to mention the significant number of people who come into software development from other fields and have never even received the inadequate computer science education that Bob was referring to.) Bob asserted that we need to apprentice these young people, these graduates and newcomers. He asserted that the most effective learning situation is one where a small number of apprentices work alongside an even smaller number of journeymen, who are receiving guidance from a master craftsman. It was music to my ears until Bob polled the audience for anyone who was working in that environment.

I proudly raised my hand, but my heart sank as I looked around and realized I was the only one raising my hand.

For the rest of the conference, I felt a sense of pride at the revelation that Obtiva's Software Studio is such a unique phenomenon. But I also struggled with a sense of sadness and

---

[*] "Red Squirrel Reflections." Available at: *http://redsquirrel.com/cgi-bin/dave/craftsmanship/a.call.for .apprenticeship.html*.

frustration at the lack of apprenticeship opportunities our industry is providing to graduates and newcomers. My biggest point of frustration is with small companies (1–20 people) made up entirely of super-experienced, world-class developers, coaches, and trainers. I understand your compulsion to only hire people with over 5 years of professional experience who have established reputations, but I believe you're hurting the industry by implicitly refusing to take on the responsibility to apprentice a few people along the way.

Where do graduates and newcomers go when they're looking for their first gig? They go where people are hiring entry level people. This is where we lose some of our greatest potential, because people who had the potential for greatness lose heart sitting at the bottom of mediocre, bloated, bureaucratic development organizations. Imagine if young Nathaniel Talbott, too inexperienced and unqualified to do much of anything interesting, had found an "entry level" position, rather than becoming the first apprentice of RoleModel Software. Sure, someone else would have probably written test/unit for Ruby. And Nathaniel would probably still have become a good software developer. But I am convinced that Nathaniel's apprenticeship made an impact on our industry, and we're better because of it.

Apprenticeship is more than simply hiring entry level people. Apprenticeship is coupling an apprentice to a journeyman. That doesn't mean they're pair programming all the time, but it does mean that the journeyman is overseeing the apprentice's progress and that the apprentice has an experienced developer in close *physical* proximity to turn to for guidance.

Furthermore, apprentices are not necessarily entry level people. Our first apprentices generally had a year or two of experience under their belt. Some are in the middle of college degrees. Some had recently graduated. One is re-booting his IT career later in life. Apprentices are people who are willing to take on a junior role that maximizes their learning opportunities, as opposed to people who try to climb as quickly as they can into roles that maximize their financial opportunities. In my experience, if the apprentice has talent and the right attitude, their financial success will inevitably follow their learning success.

Please consider creating an apprenticeship at your organization. I believe apprenticeship is our industry's best hope for addressing our talent shortage.

> I was lucky enough to attend a great university, where I learned much theory (there was less theory back then). What really made the experience shine, however, was an apprenticeship that I served. One of the graduate students took me under his wing. He didn't explicitly teach me, but he showed me by example how a great programmer thinks. Working next to him month after month, I absorbed more practical knowledge about design, coding, and debugging than any course could impart.

> Later, I joined a start-up in London where I served a different sort of apprenticeship. My new boss showed me that software development was as [much] about people as it was about technology. He helped me understand the business side of the equation and taught me how great development builds personal relationships from a base of technical strength.

I "graduated" from these two very different apprenticeships a far, far better developer than I started out. Based on my personal experience, I'm a believer. Working with masters is the best way to learn a craft.

—Dave Thomas in Pete McBreen's *Software Craftsmanship*, p. xiv

A Retrospective on the First Year of Obtiva's Apprenticeship Program

Dave Hoover

NOTE

I posted this on my blog* on March 23, 2008. After my call to action the previous year, this was my attempt to lead by example and share the hits and misses in my own attempt to establish an apprenticeship program at Obtiva. Since writing this retrospective, we have taken on two new apprentices after promoting two of our existing apprentices.

One year ago I stopped doing full-time on-site consulting. I started on-site consulting in 2004 when I joined ThoughtWorks, and continued through my first client at Obtiva. I have done a few multi-day, local stints since Spring 2007, but the vast majority of my days have been spent in a smallish office about a mile from my house in Wheaton, Illinois, USA. It was a risk to start Obtiva's Craftsmanship Studio and subsequent Apprenticeship Program, but after a ton of hard work, frequent mistakes, and mismanagement, I can confidently say these last 12 months have paid off and the future is brilliant. Let me try to explain what I'm talking about, and why I'm confident about our first year's success. (And thank you to Michael Hunger for asking for more information on this topic.)

What is a Craftsmanship Studio? I should rephrase that to "What is Obtiva's Craftsmanship Studio?" because I can only speak with authority on that. First, what does "Craftsmanship" mean in this context? My best answer to that question is to advise you to go read Part 3 of *Software Craftsmanship* by Pete McBreen. Being a self-taught programmer, and coming from a

---

* "Red Squirrel Reflections." Available at: *http://redsquirrel.com/cgi-bin/dave/obtiva/apprenticeship .program.first.year.html*.

right-brained background, the concept of craftsmanship immediately resonated with me. It should come as no surprise that when I had the opportunity to create my own practice within Obtiva, I tried to model it after the ideals that inspired me in Pete McBreen's book.

Second, what is a "Studio" in this context? The dictionary tells us that a studio is "an artist's workroom" or "an establishment where an art is taught or studied". That sounded right to me, and it is supported by the fact that Computer Programming as an Art has been a strong theme among the leaders in our field for a long time.

The above ideas basically summed up the vision for our Craftsmanship Studio: a place where programming newcomers can come to learn the craft of software development on real-world projects working closely with experienced developers. Reality was much messier than our vision, and there were too many times when apprentices were isolated or working together without much oversight. This messiness can be attributed to the fact that I am a journeyman, not a master craftsman, and therefore this year was filled with mistakes as I learned (by trial-and-error) about project management, customer relations, capacity planning, and recruiting. Thankfully we have had about 50 retrospectives during that time and have adapted our agile principles into a process that continues to improve each week.

So if our Craftsmanship Studio is where newcomers and old-timers work, learn, and mentor, what is an Apprentice? Part 3 of Pete's book will quickly introduce you to the concept of apprenticeship:

> A central tenet of the craft model is that it is hard to pick up a skill just by being told about it. You actually have to practice the skill under realistic conditions and under the watchful eye of an experienced practitioner who is providing feedback.

This describes the need and the relationship, but in reality, who are these people, these supposed newcomers? My working definition for someone in an apprenticeship is: a person who is looking to maximize their learning opportunities, even at the cost of other opportunities. Often this means purposely putting yourself into a Be The Worst situation, which is exactly what I did when I joined ThoughtWorks. For Obtiva, this means we're looking at potential and attitude rather than credentials. These people could probably make more money somewhere else in the short-term, but they are making an investment in learning that will pay off in the long-term.

I would like to see our Apprenticeship Program mature into a more formal apprenticeship with better feedback mechanisms and milestones. That said, I can say that the four apprentices who have participated in our Craftsmanship Studio have been very successful despite my shortcomings as a manager. This year reinforced for me what I learned when I was an apprentice: your apprenticeship is what you make of it. We had a Perl web developer come to us, learn Ruby and Rails and Java, and leave us writing a multi-threaded Ruby/JRuby/Java/JNI application that leveraged a 16 core machine for a local hedge fund. We had someone come to us to reboot his career, learn Unix, MySQL, Perl, Ruby and Rails and is now both managing and developing e-commerce deliveries for the Studio's largest client. We had someone come to us from a local Rails sweatshop, learn technologies like Sphinx, rSpec, god, ActiveMerchant, CruiseControl.rb, along with Perl, who is now introducing Git into the team and will soon be technical lead on his third Rails e-commerce project. We had a network administrator come to us, who after rapidly delivering several different Rails projects, is now wrangling a large, chaotic Rails codebase under control via rSpec better than many experienced developers I know.

What do I attribute our success to?

- Co-location: Nothing beats face-to-face teamwork
- Pair programming: Nothing beats side-by-side development
- Test-driven development: Nothing beats ping pong programming with tiny feedback loops
- Agile principles: Constantly re-evaluating our reality with the principles we hold and readjusting our process accordingly
- Respecting our customers: We work directly with the Goal Donor (often the same person as the Gold Owner) and use their language to build user stories
- Great tools: We use Macs with extra flatscreens and regularly bring in new technologies to boost productivity
- Hard work: Staying focused on our deliveries despite tough conditions
- Culture: Nothing beats an impromptu team snowball fight in the parking lot to get those creative juices flowing

All of these have added up to an ever-increasing demand for our services, which we are getting gradually better at managing, which combined, keeps everything chugging along at a sustainable pace. This pace is the critical piece because it means we also have lives outside the office that can energize us for our next day of teamwork.

Online Resources

- The website for this book: *http://softwarecraftsmanship.oreilly.com/wiki*
- The catalog page for this book at O'Reilly Media: *http://oreilly.com/catalog/9780596518387/*
- Software Craftsmanship mailing list: *http://groups.google.co.uk/group/software_craftsmanship*
- The Agile Manifesto: *http://agilemanifesto.org/*
- The Software Craftsmanship Manifesto: *http://manifesto.softwarecraftsmanship.org/*
- Software Craftsmanship Conference: *http://parlezuml.com/softwarecraftsmanship/*
- Software Craftsmanship North America Conference: *http://scna.softwarecraftsmanship.org/*
- Software Craftsmanship on Wikipedia: *http://en.wikipedia.org/wiki/Software_Craftsmanship*
- The Extreme Tuesday Club: *http://www.xpdeveloper.net/*
- The C2 wiki: *http://c2.com/cgi/wiki?FrontPage*
- Ade's page on the C2 wiki: *http://c2.com/cgi/wiki?AdewaleOshineye*
- Dave's page on the C2 wiki: *http://c2.com/cgi/wiki?DaveHoover*
- The Bookshelved wiki: *http://bookshelved.org/cgi-bin/wiki.pl?FrontPage*
- Ade's page on the Bookshelved wiki: *http://bookshelved.org/cgi-bin/wiki.pl?AdewaleOshineye*
- Dave's page on the Bookshelved wiki: *http://bookshelved.org/cgi-bin/wiki.pl?DaveHoover*

BIBLIOGRAPHY

[Alexander] Alexander, Christopher. *The Timeless Way of Building*. Oxford University Press, 1979.

[Alexander2] Alexander, Christopher, Sara Ishikawa, and Murray Silverstein. *A Pattern Language: Towns, Buildings, Construction*. Oxford University Press, 1977.

[Armour] Armour, Phillip G. *The Five Orders of Ignorance*. Communications of the ACM, October 2000.

[Beck] Beck, Kent. *Extreme Programming Explained: Embrace Change*. Addison-Wesley, 2004.

[Beck2] Beck, Kent. *Test-Driven Development: By Example*. Addison-Wesley, 2000.

[Becker] Becker, Howard S. *A School Is a Lousy Place to Learn Anything In*. American Behavioral Scientist, September/October 1972.

[Bentley] Bentley, Jon. *Programming Pearls*. Addison-Wesley, 1999.

[Bentley2] Bentley, Jon. *More Programming Pearls: Confessions of a Coder*. Addison-Wesley, 1998.

[Brooks] Brooks, Frederick P. *The Mythical Man Month: Essays on Software Engineering*. Addison-Wesley, 1995.

[Brown] Brown, Jr., H. Jackson. *Life's Little Instruction Book*. Thomas Nelson, 2000.

[Coplien] Coplien, James, and Neil Harrison. *Organizational Patterns of Agile Software Development*. Prentice Hall, 2004.

[Constantine] Constantine, Larry. *The Peopleware Papers: Notes on the Human Side of Software*. Prentice Hall, 2001.

[DeMarco] DeMarco, Tom, and Timothy Lister. *Peopleware: Productive Projects and Teams*. Dorset House Publishing, 1999.

[Dweck] Dweck, Carol S. *Mindset: The New Psychology of Success*. Ballantine Books, 2007.

[Dweck2] Dweck, Carol S. *Self-theories: Their Role in Motivation, Personality, and Development*. Psychology Press, 2000.

[Ericsson] Ericsson, K. Anders, Ralf Th. Krampe, and Clemens Tesch-Romer. *The Role of Deliberate Practice in the Acquisition of Expert Performance*. Psychological Review, 1993.

[Farleigh] Farleigh, John. *Fifteen Craftsmen on Their Crafts*. The Sylvan Press, 1945.

[Fowler] Fowler, Martin, Kent Beck, John Brant, William Opdyke, and Don Roberts. *Refactoring: Improving the Design of Existing Code*. Addison-Wesley, 1999.

[Gamma] Gamma, Erich, Richard Helm, Ralph Johnson, and John M. Vlissides. *Design Patterns: Elements of Reusable Object-Oriented Software*. Addison-Wesley, 1994.

[Gawande] Gawande, Atul. *Better: A Surgeon's Notes on Performance*. Metropolitan Books, 2007.

[Graham] Graham, Paul. *Hackers & Painters: Big Ideas from the Computer Age*. O'Reilly Media, 2004.

[Highsmith] Highsmith, Jim. *Agile Software Development Ecosystems*. Addison-Wesley, 2002.

[Hoffer] Hoffer, Eric. *Reflections on the Human Condition*. Hopewell Publications, 2006.

[Hunt] Hunt, Andy. *Pragmatic Thinking and Learning: Refactor Your Wetware*. Pragmatic Bookshelf, 2008.

[Jeffries] Jeffries, Ron, Ann Anderson, and Chet Hendrickson. *Extreme Programming Installed*. Addison-Wesley, 2000.

[Kerievsky] Kerievsky, Joshua. *Refactoring to Patterns*. Addison-Wesley, 2004.

[Kerth] Kerth, Norman L. *Project Retrospectives: A Handbook for Team Reviews*. Dorset House Publishing, 2001.

[Knuth] Knuth, Donald. *Computer Programming as an Art*. Communications of the ACM, 1974.

[Kruger] Kruger, Justin, and David Dunning. *Unskilled and Unaware of It: How Difficulties in Recognizing One's Own Incompetence Lead to Inflated Self-Assessments*. Journal of Personality and Social Psychology, 1999.

[Lammers] Lammers, Susan. *Programmers at Work: Interviews With 19 Programmers Who Shaped the Computer Industry*. Tempus Books, 1989.

[Lave] Lave, Jean, and Etienne Wenger. *Situated Learning: Legitimate Peripheral Participation*. Cambridge University Press, 1991.

[Leonard] Leonard, George. *Mastery: The Keys to Success and Long-Term Fulfillment*. Plume, 1992.

[Lewis] Lewis, C. S. *The Weight of Glory and Other Addresses*. HarperOne, 2001.

[McBreen] McBreen, Pete. *Software Craftsmanship: The New Imperative*. Addison-Wesley, 2001.

[McConnell] McConnell, Steve. *Code Complete: A Practical Handbook of Software Construction*. Microsoft Press, 2004.

[Meyer] Meyer, Bertrand. *Object-Oriented Software Construction*. Prentice Hall, 2000.

[Peter] Peter, Laurence J, Raymond Hull, and Robert I Sutton. *The Peter Principle: Why Things Always Go Wrong*. HarperBusiness, 2009.

[Pirsig] Pirsig, Robert. *Zen and the Art of Motorcycle Maintenance: An Inquiry into Values*. Harper Perennial Modern Classics, 2008.

[Postrel] Postrel, Virginia. *The Future and Its Enemies: The Growing Conflict over Creativity, Enterprise and Progress*. Free Press, 1999.

[Rogers] Rogers, Carl, and Peter D Kramer. *On Becoming a Person: A Therapist's View of Psychotherapy*. Mariner Books, 1995.

[Sennet] Sennet, Richard. *The Craftsman*. Yale University Press, 2009.

[Skiena] Skiena, Steven S. *The Algorithm Design Manual*. Springer, 2008.

[Sudo] Sudo, Philip. *Zen Guitar*. Simon & Schuster, 1998.

[Surowiecki] Surowiecki, James. *The Wisdom of Crowds*. Anchor, 2005.

[Suzuki] Suzuki, Shunryu. *Zen Mind, Beginner's Mind*. Shambhala, 2006.

[Tharp] Tharp, Twyla, and Mark Reiter. *The Creative Habit: Learn It and Use It for Life*. Simon & Schuster, 2005.

[Thomas] Thomas, Dave, and Andy Hunt. *The Pragmatic Programmer: From Journeyman to Master*. Addison-Wesley, 1999.

[Tractate] *Tractate Avot (f (http://www.jewishvirtuallibrary.org/jsource/Talmud/avot4.html))*.

[Vlissides] Vlissides, John M. *Pattern Hatching: Design Patterns Applied*. Addison-Wesley, 1998.

[Wall] Wall, Larry, Tom Christiansen, and Jon Orwant. *Programming Perl*. O'Reilly Media, 2000.

[Weick] Weick, Karl E, and Karlene H. Roberts. *Collective Mind in Organizations: Heedful Interrelating on Flight Decks*. Administrative Science Quarterly, 1993.

[Weinberg] Weinberg, Gerald M. *Becoming a Technical Leader: An Organic Problem-Solving Approach*. Dorset House Publishing, 1986.

[Weinberg2] Weinberg, Gerald M. *More Secrets of Consulting: The Consultant's Tool Kit*. Dorset House Publishing, 2001.

[Weinberg3] Weinberg, Gerald M. *The Psychology of Computer Programming: Silver Anniversary Edition*. Dorset House Publishing, 1998.

[Wetherell] Wetherell, Charles. *Etudes for Programmers*. Prentice Hall, 1978.

[Williams] Williams, Laurie. *Pair Programming Illuminated*. Addison-Wesley, 2002.

[Whitehead] Whitehead, Alfred North. *An Introduction to Mathematics*. BiblioLife, 2009.

INDEX

humility, 71
Hunt, Andy, 18, 74

I

identifying errors, 94
ignorance
    confronting, 28
    exposing, 26

J

Jeffries, Ron, 38
job titles, 51
Jobs, Steve, 45
Johnson, Ralph, 16
journeymen, 4, 7

K

katas, 78
Kerievsky, Joshua, 101, 104
Kerth, Norm, 85
Kindred Spirits pattern, 64
Knuth, Donald, 79
Kruger, Justin, 92
Kua, Patrick, 93

L

Lave, Jean, 70
Learn How You Fail pattern, 94
learning
    increasing the pace, 74
    sandboxes, 15
Leonard, George, 19, 38, 47, 52, 62, 77
Lewis, C.S., 73
The Long Road pattern, 38
long-term planning, 39

M

Mahler, Gustaf, 37
maintaining confidence, 33
    certifications, 38
"Maps of People's Personal Practices" web page, 86
Martin, Robert, 78
masters and mastery, 7
McAdam, Desi, 49
McBreen, Pete, 3, 8, 22
McConnell, Steve, 106
McMahon, Chris, 49
mentors, 16, 62
Merritt, Eric, 17
Metheny, Pat, 59
Mohan, Ravi, 101

Morris, Chris, xii, 59
motivation, 43
    potential barriers, 43
    promotion and, 52

N

National Lottery number set generator, 20

O

online resources, 131
Oshineye, Ade, xvi, 15
O'Reilly, Tim, 75

P

Pagel, Paul, 69
pair programming, 86
passion, 46
pattern forms, xiv
pattern languages, xiv, 9
Pattern Languages of Programs workshop website, xiii
pattern list, 119
patterns, xiii
perlmonks, 38
perpetual learning, 74
personal practices maps, 86
Peter Principle, 85
Pirsig, Robert, 33, 99
practice, 77
    building toy systems, 80
programming languages
    assessing language differences, 17
    building on prior knowledge, 19–21
    idioms, 16, 18
    learning a first language, 14
        language specifications, 18
        mentors, 16
        small steps, 15
promotion and your goals, 52

R

Radhakrishnan, Mohan, 47
reading lists, 100
    finding classics, 104
recognition, 51
Record What You Learn pattern, 88
reflection, 85
Retreat into Competence pattern, 33
review, 88
Riepenhausen, Enrique Comba, 31
Roberts, Karlene, 23
Rogers, Carl, 28
Rubbing Elbows pattern, 66

Dave Hoover, Obtiva's Chief Craftsman, enjoys developing software developers while developing software. He specializes in delivering projects for entrepreneurs.

Adewale Oshineye, an engineer at Google, has worked on projects ranging from point-of-sale systems for electrical retailers to trading systems for investment banks.

COLOPHON

Our look is the result of reader comments, our own experimentation, and feedback from distribution channels. Distinctive covers complement our distinctive approach to technical topics, breathing personality and life into potentially dry subjects.

The cover image is from Corbis (*http://pro.corbis.com/*). The cover font is Adobe ITC Garamond. The text font is Linotype Birka; the heading font is Adobe Myriad Condensed; and the code font is LucasFont's TheSansMonoCondensed.

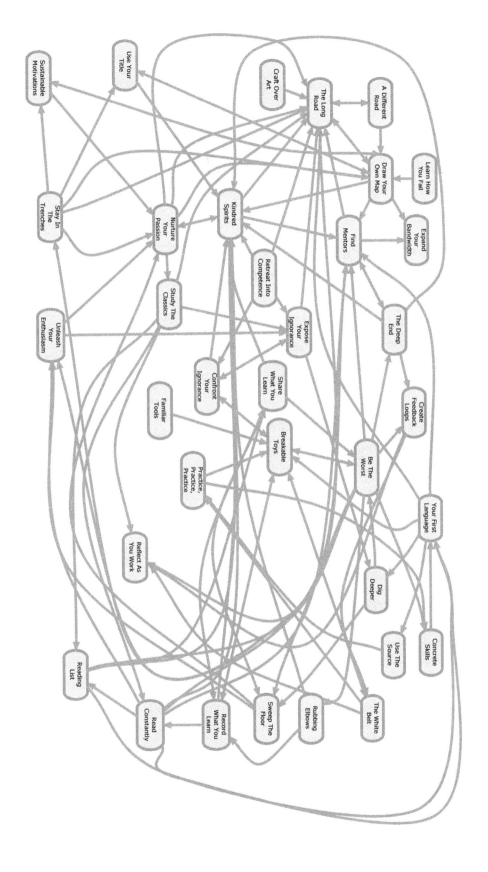

Get even more for your money.

Join the O'Reilly Community, and register the O'Reilly books you own. It's free, and you'll get:

- $4.99 ebook upgrade offer
- 40% upgrade offer on O'Reilly print books
- Membership discounts on books and events
- Free lifetime updates to ebooks and videos
- Multiple ebook formats, DRM FREE
- Participation in the O'Reilly community
- Newsletters
- Account management
- 100% Satisfaction Guarantee

Signing up is easy:

1. **Go to: oreilly.com/go/register**
2. **Create an O'Reilly login.**
3. **Provide your address.**
4. **Register your books.**

Note: English-language books only

To order books online:
oreilly.com/store

For questions about products or an order:
orders@oreilly.com

To sign up to get topic-specific email announcements and/or news about upcoming books, conferences, special offers, and new technologies:
elists@oreilly.com

For technical questions about book content:
booktech@oreilly.com

To submit new book proposals to our editors:
proposals@oreilly.com

O'Reilly books are available in multiple DRM-free ebook formats. For more information:
oreilly.com/ebooks

O'REILLY®

Spreading the knowledge of innovators · oreilly.com

Have it your way.

Milton Keynes UK
Ingram Content Group UK Ltd.
UKHW051205110923
428458UK00003B/3